Getting rich with Jeremy James

David Henry Wilson was educated at Dulwich College and Pembroke College, Cambridge, where he read Modern Languages. He has lived in France, Ghana, Germany and Switzerland, and now holds a senior academic post at Konstanz University, West Germany, though by special arrangement he does most of his teaching at Bristol University. He has had several plays performed in England, Germany and America, and is the author of several popular children's books about the irrepressible Jeremy James. His first book, *Elephants don't sit on cars*, was published with equal success in Germany where it was featured on radio and television. David Henry Wilson is married, with three children, and lives in Taunton, Somerset.

Getting rich with Jeremy James

by David Henry Wilson

illustrated by Patricia Drew

Piccolo Books

First published 1979 by Chatto & Windus Ltd
This Piccolo edition published 1984 by Pan Books Ltd,
Cavaye Place, London SW10 9PG
9 8 7 6 5 4
© David Henry Wilson 1979
illustrations © Patricia Drew 1979
ISBN 0 330 28383 9
Phototypeset by Input Typesetting Ltd, London
Printed and bound in Great Britain by
Cox & Wyman Ltd, Reading

For Lisbeth,
with love

Contents

Daddy's new car

Daddy had bought a new car. It was not a *new* new car, but a second-hand new car – in fact, an old second-hand new car. But although it was old, it was not as old as Daddy's old car, which had been very old indeed, and which Jeremy James had once seen an elephant sit on. Cars are not really designed to be sat on by elephants, and Daddy's old car had not been designed to be sat on by anything. Mummy said it was more of an ornament than a car, because it spent most of its time standing very still, either in the street outside or in the repair-shop. When it did move, it was usually on the end of a rope, being pulled along by the van from the repair-shop. Anyway, when the twins were born it was obvious that the family were going to need a bigger car (not to mention a car that could move), and so Daddy sold the old old car and bought the new old car.

It was a moment of great excitement when Daddy pulled up outside the house in a long blue limousine that shone like a new pair of shoes. He gave a toot on the hooter (which sounded much grander than the honk of the old car), and Mummy and Jeremy James rushed out of the house to inspect the new arrival, while the twins were left in their cots to inspect the ceiling or each other.

'It's lovely,' said Mummy. 'It looks almost new!'

'Only done forty thousand miles,' said Daddy.

'That sounds a lot to me,' said Mummy.

'Not for a car,' said Daddy.

'How much did our old one do, Daddy?' asked Jeremy James.

'Never more than two yards at a time,' said Daddy. 'Come on, get the twins and we'll go for a run.'

Jeremy James wondered why they should go running when they'd just got a new car, but as they'd often gone walking when they'd had the old car, he assumed this was just the way grown-ups did things. In any case he had no time to ask as Mummy whisked him back into the house to get his coat on, and then went upstairs with Daddy to get Christopher and Jennifer ready.

'Let's go out into the country,' said Mummy.

'Or I could take her on the motorway,' said Daddy. 'Get up a bit of speed.'

'The country would be nicer,' said Mummy. 'And we can stop off somewhere for tea.'

Jeremy James pricked up his ears. He liked stopping off somewhere for tea. Platefuls of strawberries hovered before his eyes . . .

'Can I have cream on them?' he asked.

'Cream on what?' said Mummy.

'On my strawberries,' said Jeremy James.

'You don't get strawberries at this time of the year,' said Mummy. 'You get hot buttered scones and toast and cakes.'

'And strawberry jam,' said Jeremy James.

'And strawberry jam if you like,' said Mummy.

'With cream on it,' said Jeremy James.

Mummy had changed Jennifer's nappy, and had wrapped her up in a clean dress and a woolly coat, and Jennifer was laughing happily. Daddy had just stabbed himself with the safety-pin on Christopher's dirty nappy, and was sucking his injured thumb while Christopher was crying.

'I'll do him,' said Mummy. 'You hold Jennifer.'

'I'd better just get some plaster on this,' said Daddy.

But eventually both twins were ready, Christopher stopped crying, Daddy's thumb was plastered, the pram had been taken apart, both parts had been loaded into the back of the new car with the twins lying cosily in the top part, and Mummy and Daddy and Jeremy James were all strapped into their seats.

'Here we go, then,' said Daddy. 'Next stop Monte Carlo.'

Daddy pressed a button, and there was a loud whirring sound. Daddy stopped pressing the button, and the loud whirring sound stopped, too. Then Daddy pressed the button again, and there was a loud whirring sound again. Daddy stopped pressing, and everything was very quiet.

'Just . . . um . . . got cold . . .' said Daddy, and pressed the button again. There was the same whirring sound, followed by the same silence.

'Could be flooded,' said Daddy. 'Unless it's overheated. I'll take a look.'

He pulled a lever, unstrapped himself, and got out. He went to the front of the car and then disappeared from view behind the raised bonnet.

'It sounded a bit like our old car, didn't it, Mummy?' said Jeremy James.

'Yes,' said Mummy. 'And it seems to go like our old car, too.'

Daddy came back.

'Can't see anything,' he said. 'I'll just give it another try.'

He sat in his seat and pressed the button. There was a loud whirring sound, followed by a loud silence.

'Perhaps you'd better give them a ring,' said Mummy.

'Hmmph!' said Daddy. 'I'll have another look.' And he got out again and disappeared again and came back again and sat down again. 'It's a lovely clean engine,' he said. 'Lovely, clean, and dead.'

'Why don't you give them a ring?' said Mummy.

'One more try,' said Daddy. 'If I can just take it by surprise.' He put his finger on the button, looked out of the window, and then suddenly pressed down. There was a loud whirring sound. Daddy kept his finger down, and the whirring sound gradually slowed till it became more of a wheezing than a whirring. Daddy took his finger off. There was silence.

'Perhaps I'd better give them a ring,' he said.

From the back of the car came a howl that was even louder than the loud whirring sound had been. Jennifer had kicked Christopher, and Christopher was much easier to start than Daddy's car. Even though Jennifer had only kicked him once, his howl motor was running at full speed.

'I'll get them back inside,' said Mummy, 'while you go to the phone-box. Do you want to stay in the car, Jeremy James?'

'Oh, yes please,' said Jeremy James.

'Right. Daddy'll be back again in a minute.'

Mummy and Daddy took a giggling Jennifer and a

wailing Christopher into the house, then Daddy set off down the road to the phone-box. Jeremy James sat quietly in his seat, gazing at the starter button, the control panel and, above all, the steering wheel of Daddy's car. How he would love to sit at the steering wheel, and swing it round, and swing it back again. And how he would love to pull the levers and press the switches and flash and hoot and brrm brrm and eeeek round corners.

With a tug and a squeeze and a wriggle, Jeremy James escaped from his straps and dived headfirst into Daddy's seat. Another little wriggle put him in just the right position, his nose level with the middle of the steering wheel. Jeremy James grasped the steering wheel firmly in both hands. 'Brrm brrm,' he said, and swung the car screeching round the bend, hot on the tail of a gang of escaped bandits. 'Eeow!' said Jeremy James, and 'Eerrk!' and 'Brrm brrm brrm!'

Then he jerked at the lever in the floor, just as he had seen Daddy do in the old car, and it clicked into a new position.

'Gosh,' said Jeremy James, 'I hope I haven't broken it!'

He waggled the lever around, but it didn't seem to be broken. It was just a little loose.

'Maybe that's how it *ought* to be,' said Jeremy James. 'Maybe that's what was wrong – Daddy had it in the wrong place!'

Jeremy James did some hard thinking. If Daddy *had* had it in the wrong place, and it was now in the right place, the car should go. And wouldn't Mummy and Daddy be pleased if the car went. They would be so pleased that they would give Jeremy James hundreds of scones and thousands of cakes and

millions of kisses. He would be a real live hero. If the car went. Jeremy James looked hard at the starter button. Jeremy James pressed the starter button. But nothing happened. There was not even a whirring sound.

Jeremy James did some more hard thinking. Perhaps the car *shouldn't* make a whirring sound. Perhaps silence was what you *ought* to hear when you pressed the button, and the loud whirring sound had been a sign that the lever in the floor was in the wrong position, only Daddy hadn't known that because, after all, this was a new car. Perhaps the car was all ready to go now the lever was in the right position.

Jeremy James tried to remember what Daddy used to do with the old car when it was ready to go. Wasn't there another lever Daddy used to pull?

Jeremy James looked for another lever. And sure enough, right behind the first lever he had pulled there was a second lever, and it had a button in it. Jeremy James smiled to himself, pressed the button, and gently lowered the second lever to the floor.

There was a creak, a little jerk, and . . . the car . . . was it? . . . yes, the car was moving! He'd done it! Oh, wouldn't Mummy and Daddy be pleased! Jeremy James lifted himself up in the seat so that he could look out of the window, and there was no doubt about it, the houses on the other side of the street were slowly slipping by in the opposite direction. In fact, they were slipping by a little faster now. In fact, even as he looked, they seemed to be gathering speed. Jeremy James stopped smiling, and his heart began to pound. He hadn't meant to go as fast as this! He took hold of the steering wheel, but then he couldn't see out of the window any more, and so he just swung the steering wheel from side to side and hoped for the best and wished he hadn't mended Daddy's car after all.

There was a loud thump and a tinkle of broken glass, and the car suddenly stopped. It stopped so suddenly that Jeremy James was thrown forward and bumped his nose hard on the middle of the steering wheel. The thump and the bump brought tears into and out of Jeremy James's eyes, and he sat at the steering wheel howling louder than the loud whirring noise and Christopher's wail put together. Then the car door opened, and there was Daddy lifting him out and holding him very tightly. And Mummy came running a moment later, and took him from Daddy, and asked if her little darling was all right, and Daddy said her little darling was all right, but his new car jolly well wasn't. Then Mummy said they shouldn't have left Jeremy James alone in the car, and Daddy said Jeremy James should have kept his hands off Daddy's new car, and Jeremy James howled very loudly because that seemed the safest thing to do.

There were soon quite a lot of people standing round Daddy's new car. Jeremy James heard their voices through Mummy's shoulder and they were saying things like 'How did it happen?' and 'Could have been killed!' and 'Who's going to pay for my garden wall?' and 'Don't worry, Mr Johnson, I'll see to everything, I'm ever so sorry . . .' The last one was definitely Daddy's voice. Then Mummy carried Jeremy James away, and he risked a little peep over the top of her shoulder. Daddy's new car was right across the pavement, with its front all squashed up against a wall, and Daddy was talking to a red-faced

man with a bristling moustache, and there was a
policeman coming up the road towards them. Jeremy
James hid his face again and let out a few more loud
sobs.

'It's all right,' said Mummy, giving him an extra
pat and a squeeze, 'don't cry. It's all right.'

Then she carried him into the house and gave him
a big piece of chocolate, which helped to dry his eyes
and silence his sobs. Chocolate was a medicine Jeremy
James always responded to very quickly.

A little while later, Mummy called him to come
and look out of the window, and she picked him up
again so that he could get a good view. The van from
the repair-shop was just going by, and it was followed
by a long rope, and on the end of the rope was
Daddy's new car, looking very crumpled. At the
steering wheel of Daddy's new car was Daddy, and
he was looking rather crumpled, too.

'Oh Mummy,' said Jeremy James, 'it looks just like the old car now.'

'Hmmph!' said Mummy, and held him very tight.

How to get rich

'How do you make money?' asked Jeremy James one morning at breakfast.

'No idea,' said Daddy. 'But if you ever find out, let me know.'

'You have to work for it,' said Mummy. 'You work, and then people pay you.'

'What sort of work?' asked Jeremy James.

'All sorts,' said Mummy. 'Different people do different work.'

'Well, what sort of work could I do to get some money?' asked Jeremy James.

'What do *you* need money for?' asked Mummy.

'Spending,' said Jeremy James.

'Spending on what?' asked Mummy.

Why was it that grown-ups never answered questions? You could ask them about anything, but they would never tell you what you wanted to know. Only yesterday he'd asked Mummy why the man they'd just walked past had one leg instead of two, and Mummy had said 'Sh!' to him as if he'd said something rude. 'I only want to know what's happened to his other leg,' Jeremy James had said, but Mummy had shushed him again with a threatening look. And the day before that, when he'd watched Mummy bathing the twins and had asked why Jennifer hadn't got something he and Christopher *had* got, all he received was a 'Hmmph!' instead of an answer. You never got answers from grown-ups. Just 'sh', 'hmmph', or questions about why you were asking questions.

'Toys,' said Jeremy James. 'So that I can buy more toys.' He would have said sweets, but toys sounded more respectable.

'Haven't you got enough toys?' said Mummy.

'Well I haven't got a tricycle with a saddlebag,' said Jeremy James. 'So how can I get money for a tricycle with a saddlebag?'

'I haven't got a tricycle with a saddlebag either,' said Daddy. 'It seems to be a common weakness in the family.'

Daddy tended not to say 'sh' or 'hmmph' or ask questions; he just said things that had nothing to do with what you were asking.

'Well, what work can I do?' asked Jeremy James, who could be very determined when he wanted to be.

'Let's have a look in the paper,' said Daddy. 'See if we can find something suitable.'

And Daddy spread the paper out at the page where it said 'Jobs Vacant'.

'Now then,' he said. 'How about "long-distance lorry-driver"? No, not after your efforts at short-distance car-driving. "Cook required part-time at nursing home." What's your cooking like, Jeremy James?'

'I'm good at strawberries and ice-cream,' said Jeremy James.

'But you'd never leave any for the patients,' said Daddy.

'That's true,' said Jeremy James. 'But I'd like that sort of work.'

20

'I expect you would,' said Daddy. 'It's the kind of job you could grow fat on. How about being a coalman?'

'Too dirty,' said Jeremy James.

'A street cleaner, then?' said Daddy.

'I don't like cleaning,' said Jeremy James.

'Ah,' said Daddy. 'So it's got to be something that won't make you dirty and won't make you clean.'

'And they must pay me lots of money,' said Jeremy James.

'Nothing like that here, I'm afraid,' said Daddy, closing the paper. 'Fairy godmothers don't advertise in our paper.'

Mummy and Daddy smiled at each other, but Jeremy James didn't think it was funny. Sweets (and toys and tricycles with saddlebags) cost money, and if you wanted money you had to work, and if you couldn't work, you couldn't have money, and without money you couldn't have sweets (or toys or tricycles with saddlebags). And that wasn't at all funny. Jeremy James frowned. And behind his frown there began to stir a vague memory from the distant past. It had been at least two days ago. He had gone round the corner with Mummy to the greengrocer's shop, and in the greengrocer's window had been a large notice which Mummy had helped him to read. 'Bright Lad Wanted' – that's what the notice had said. Jeremy James thought hard for a moment.

'Mummy,' said Jeremy James. 'Am I bright?'

'As bright as a button,' said Mummy.

Jeremy James thought hard for another moment.

'Daddy,' said Jeremy James. 'How much do bright lads get paid?'

'Depends what they're doing,' said Daddy.

'Sort of . . . well . . . greengrocering?' said Jeremy James.

'No idea,' said Daddy. 'I expect they get the union rates for bright greengrocering lads.'

'What's union rates?' asked Jeremy James.

'That's what you'll get paid when you get that job,' said Daddy.

Jeremy James did some more hard thinking. The problem was not what to do, but how to get permission to do it. He looked at Mummy, and he looked at Daddy, and he looked at the table, and he took a deep breath and said: 'Can I just go round the corner to the . . . um . . . sweetshop?'

To his surprise, Mummy gave him permission without asking a single question.

'Good luck!' said Daddy, as Jeremy James left the house.

'But don't go into the road,' said Mummy, 'and come straight home afterwards.'

Jeremy James walked proudly and brightly up the street and round the corner to the greengrocer's shop. The notice was still in the window. Jeremy James puffed out his chest, and marched in.

'And what can we do for you?' asked a thin man in a brown coat, with a face like a wizened apple.

'I'm a bright lad,' said Jeremy James.

'Aha!' said the wizened apple, 'I can see that. But what can I do for you?'

'Well I've come for the job,' said Jeremy James. 'So that I can get enough money for a tricycle with a saddlebag. And you should pay me onion rates.'

'Onion rates, eh?' said the man in the brown coat. 'What's your name, then, sonny?'

'Jeremy James,' said Jeremy James.

'That's a smart-sounding name all right,' said the man in the brown coat. 'But to tell you the truth, Jeremy James, we were really looking for someone a little older and a little bigger.'

'I'll be getting bigger,' said Jeremy James. 'I've grown quite a lot since last week.'

'Oh you'll be growing fast, I'm sure,' said the man. 'You'll be growing at onion rates, won't you? But you see, we need someone to carry big loads of fruit and vegetables around. And he'd have to be able to carry them on a bicycle to the houses around here.'

'Well I could put them in my saddlebag,' said Jeremy James. 'When I've got a saddlebag.'

'And when you've got a tricycle,' said the man.

'Yes,' said Jeremy James.

'No, I don't think that would work,' said the man. 'Because there's an awful lot to carry.'

'I'll get a *big* saddlebag,' said Jeremy James, not too hopefully.

'In any case,' said the man, 'you couldn't do the job till you had your tricycle. And you can't have your tricycle till you've done the job. It's what's called a vicious circle. Or cycle.'

Jeremy James's head dropped down on his chest like a cabbage too heavy for its stalk.

'I'll tell you what,' said the man. 'You try and grow nice and quickly, and when you're as tall as my shoulder, come back and I'll give you the job.'

'I'll never be as tall as your shoulder,' said Jeremy James.

'If you eat plenty of fresh fruit and vegetables,' said the man, 'you'll be up past my shoulder in no time. And I'll start you off myself, how's that? Come here, Jeremy James. Now take this paper bag.'

Jeremy James took the large paper bag that the man held out to him.

'Now you go round my shop,' said the man, 'and fill that paper bag with anything you like.'

'Anything?' said Jeremy James.

'Anything,' said the man.

Jeremy James looked round the shop. Apples, oranges, pears, bananas . . . potatoes, tomatoes, beans, carrots . . .

'You haven't got any chocolate, have you?' said Jeremy James.

'Afraid not,' said the man.

'Or any tins of mandarin oranges?' asked Jeremy James.

'No tins here,' said the man. 'Everything fresh as God made it.'

Jeremy James filled his bag until its sides were splitting and he needed both hands and both arms to hold it all together.

'Off you go, then, Jeremy James,' said the man, 'and I'll see you when you're up to my shoulder.'

'All right,' said Jeremy James. 'I'll be back next week. Thank you very much for the bagful.'

When Mummy and Daddy saw the bag of fruit, their eyes opened as wide as apples and pears.

'Where did that come from?' asked Mummy.

'I went for a job at the greengrocer's,' said Jeremy James.

'Did you get it?' asked Daddy.

'Well, not exactly,' said Jeremy James. 'He said I should come back next week when I'm as tall as his shoulder.'

'Ah,' said Daddy, 'and he gave you all this to help you grow.'

'Yes,' said Jeremy James, 'I'll be growing at onion rates.'

'Well, that is a lovely lot of fruit,' said Mummy, emptying the bag on to the table. 'Worth a small fortune.'

An idea came into Jeremy James's mind, and lit up his eyes from inside.

'Well, it is mine,' he said, 'but you can have it for nothing if you give me some money for it.'

Mummy looked at Daddy, and Daddy looked at Mummy.

'Fair enough,' said Daddy. 'If you want free fruit, you must pay for it.'

'How much are you asking?' said Mummy.

'It's worth a small fortune,' said Jeremy James. 'But I'd like enough to buy a tricycle with a saddlebag.'

'Oh,' said Mummy, 'now that would be a large fortune.'

'All right,' said Jeremy James. 'Enough for a box of liquorice all-sorts.'

And to Jeremy James's surprise and delight, Mummy agreed. Ten minutes later Jeremy James was hurrying back up the road and round the corner to the sweetshop, and on his face was a smile as wide as a banana. It was the smile of a man who had done a good day's work.

The christening

Christopher and Jennifer were to be christened. Jeremy James found the idea of christening a little difficult to understand. Mummy explained to him that the twins would be named and dipped in water, but Jeremy James pointed out that they already had names and that Mummy dipped them in water every day, so why did they have to go to church to be given names they already had and a bath which they wouldn't need? Then Mummy said Jesus wanted little children to be christened, but Jeremy James reckoned Jesus couldn't have known the twins had already been given their names and their bath. Then Mummy said Jeremy James was too young to understand but he could look forward to the party afterwards, and Jeremy James decided that if there was going to be a party afterwards, maybe christenings were a good thing after all and Jesus knew what he was doing.

There were not many people in the church, which seemed all dusty and hollow, and the people who *were* there talked in very quiet voices, as if they were afraid to wake somebody up.

'Mummy,' said Jeremy James in a loud voice that echoed round the walls of the church, 'why is everybody whispering?'

One or two heads turned in Jeremy James's direction and Mummy's face went a little red.

'Because,' whispered Mummy, 'you're not supposed to talk loudly in church.'

Mummy looked very smart in a blue suit with a flowery blue hat, and she was holding Christopher, who was wrapped up in a soft blue shawl. Christopher was peeping round him, and didn't seem to like what he saw. There was a slightly alarmed expression in his eyes, and his lips were turned down at both ends. Although the sun shone brightly outside the church, there was a distinct threat of showers inside.

Daddy also looked very smart in his grey suit with a neat grey and white tie. He was holding a pink-shawled Jennifer, who giggled loudly as Daddy tickled her under the chin. Daddy had to stop tickling her, because Jennifer didn't understand that you weren't supposed to make loud noises in church.

And between Mummy and Daddy stood Jeremy James, in a suit as grey as Daddy's, with his face scrubbed clean and his hair well brushed and parted. He gazed round the high, hollow church, and wondered why God chose to live in such a gloomy place. He reckoned God would be a lot happier if someone were to stick paper chains across His ceiling.

As Jeremy James gazed and pondered, the door of the church opened and in came Uncle Jack, Aunt Janet, and Melissa, who was the same age as Jeremy James. Uncle Jack and Aunt Janet caught sight of Mummy and Daddy, and gave them a cheerful wave. Melissa caught sight of Jeremy James and stuck out her tongue. Jeremy James screwed up his face, put his thumb to his nose, and waggled his fingers. Just as he did so, the Reverend Cole hobbled up the aisle and drew level with Mummy.

'Ah, good morning!' said the Reverend Cole in a hollow creaky voice, and peered short-sightedly at Mummy. 'You must be . . . ah yes, of course . . . and this is . . .'

'Christopher,' said Mummy, 'and my husband's holding Jennifer.'

'That's right,' said the Reverend Cole, 'Christopher and Jennifer . . . I must remember that.' Then the Reverend Cole peered short-sightedly at Jeremy James. 'And what's this little girl's name?'

'Jeremy James,' said Jeremy James. 'But . . .'

'Jeremy James,' said the Reverend Cole, bending his tall thin body over like a hairpin, 'that's an unusual name for a little girl.'

'I'm a little boy,' said Jeremy James.

'Ah, that explains it,' said the Reverend Cole. 'Now when it's time, I want you and your family and friends to come to the back and gather round the font. All right? You can't miss it. So nice to see you. Christopher and Jennifer . . . two for the price of one, eh?'

And the Reverend Cole hobbled away to begin the service. The Reverend Cole always hobbled, because he was very old and his legs were very rubbery, but today his hobble was mixed with a wobble because yesterday, quite by accident, he had sat on a wasp and the wasp had stung him. The wasp, of course, had died, but the Reverend Cole had been left with a sore bottom.

When the service began, the Reverend Cole spoke out in a very loud voice, though Jeremy James wasn't sure what he was saying. Jeremy James whispered to Mummy that she should tell the man he wasn't supposed to talk loudly in church, but Mummy said

'Sh!', and just then everybody started singing at the tops of their voices: 'Blessed Jesus, here we stand.' One moment you had to be very quiet and the next moment you had to be very loud – that was typical grown-up topsy-turvy. 'Blessed Jesus, here we stand,' they sang, as if Jesus didn't know already.

At last, after more singing, talking, mumbling, and one long silence when everybody was supposed to close his eyes but Jeremy James didn't and nothing happened to him, the Reverend Cole eased himself out of the pulpit and trod painfully up the aisle.

As Mummy and Daddy were carrying the babies, they had to be very close to the Reverend Cole and the big stone saucer in which the twins were to take their bath. There was no room for Jeremy James as well, and so he found himself standing just behind the tall stooping figure of the Reverend Cole. On the other side of the Reverend Cole stood Uncle Jack and Aunt Janet, and behind them, exactly level with Jeremy James, was Cousin Melissa. She was wearing pigtails and a red and white spotted dress, and she was carrying a doll with pigtails and a red and white spotted dress, and she thought she looked pretty but Jeremy James didn't think she looked pretty. Jeremy James thought she looked ugly. And he thought her doll looked ugly, too. It was a job to decide which was uglier, Melissa or her doll. 'You both look ugly,' whispered Jeremy James to Melissa, and pulled the doll's pigtail.

'Stop it!' said Melissa, in a loud voice. Heads turned.

'Sh!' said Aunt Janet, with a frown.

'Jennifer, I baptise thee in the name of the Father

and of the Son and of the Holy Spirit. Amen,' said the Reverend Cole, and bent over the font like a giraffe picking daisies. He sprinkled her with water, and she came up smiling.

'Aaaah!' said several voices at once, as the Reverend Cole handed her back to a proud Daddy.

'You're smelly,' whispered Jeremy James to Melissa.

'So are you,' whispered Melissa to Jeremy James.

'Not as smelly as you,' whispered Jeremy James to Melissa.

Mummy handed Christopher over to the Reverend Cole. He was scarcely halfway across when the thunderstorm broke. Tears rained from his eyes and a piercing howl gusted out of his wide-open mouth. A shudder ran through the assembly, and the Reverend Cole thought seriously of retirement.

'Your doll is as ugly and smelly as you are,' whispered Jeremy James to Melissa.

'I'm going to tell on you,' said Melissa to Jeremy James.

'Just like a girl,' said Jeremy James to Melissa, and this time he pulled one of Melissa's pigtails.

'You stop it!' cried Melissa, and gave Jeremy James a good hard push.

As Jeremy James had had to lean over to pull Melissa's pigtail, he was off balance when she pushed him. He staggered, and he would certainly have fallen if he hadn't managed to hold on to the nearest support. The nearest support was the Reverend Cole, and as the Reverend Cole was at that moment bending over the font to give Christopher his bath, Jeremy James grasped the very part of the Reverend

Cole on which the dead wasp had chosen to make its mark.

'Christopher, I baptise thee in the name of the Faaaaaaaaaah!' cried the Reverend Cole, and dropped the howling Christopher straight into the font. Mummy swiftly scooped her wet and wailing baby out of the water, the Reverend Cole stood trembling, with one hand clasped to his bottom and the other flapping uselessly in the air, Daddy gaped and Jennifer gurgled, and Jeremy James quickly squeezed in between Mummy and Daddy and stood very still, gazing up at the font.

'Oh dear . . . most unfortunate . . . lively little fellow . . .' said the Reverend Cole. 'Um . . . perhaps you'd better hold him now . . .'

By the time the Reverend Cole had finished the service, Christopher's squalls had died down into occasional sobs, though they did flare up again when the Reverend Cole muttered, 'There's a good boy,' and tried to pat him on the head. And, by the time they all got home, he had fallen into a deep healing sleep, which Mummy piously thanked Heaven for.

The party was a great success. Jeremy James handed round platefuls of sandwiches and cakes and showed everyone how to eat them, Melissa was sick, and Uncle Jack and two other uncles each gave Jeremy James ten pence on their way out. Jeremy James reckoned that Jesus really did know what he was doing when he invented christenings.

'Could have been quite nasty,' said Daddy, when everyone had gone and they were left with nothing but memories and dirty dishes.

'What on earth made him shout like that?' said

Mummy. 'And fancy dropping poor Christopher in the font!'

'He's obviously past it,' said Daddy. 'Should be made to lie down in green pastures if you ask me.'

'Anyway,' said Mummy, 'everything else went well. And I thought Jeremy James was a very good boy today.'

Daddy put his arm round his big son. 'That's true,' he said. 'Never heard a word from him right through the service. There'll be a bonus on your pocket money this week, my boy.'

Jeremy James gave a big smile, and gazed innocently up at his proud Mummy and Daddy. The fact that grown-ups live in a topsy-turvy world can sometimes have its advantages.

Timothy's birthday party

Timothy was the little boy who lived in the big house next door. He was a year older than Jeremy James, and he knew everything there was to know, and he had everything there was to have. Timothy went to school, though Jeremy James wasn't quite sure whether Timothy went there as a pupil or as a teacher, since he knew such a lot. And although on every day of the year Timothy was more important than anybody else, today he was doubly more important, because today was his birthday. He had long ago invited all his friends to the best birthday party they would ever be lucky enough to attend, and Jeremy James was one of the chosen few.

'Ding-dong!' said the front doorbell of Timothy's house, and a moment later the door had opened and there stood Timothy's Mummy.

'Hello, Mrs Smyth-Forcitick,' said Jeremy James. (The name was Smyth-Fortescue, but Jeremy James couldn't quite get his tongue in the right position.)

'Ah, hello, Jeremy,' said Mrs Smyth-Fortescue.

'Jeremy *James*,' said Jeremy James.

'That's right. Do come in, Jeremy.'

And a moment later, Jeremy James was face to face with the great hero himself.

'Happy birthday, Tim,' said Jeremy James, handing over a large box-shaped parcel wrapped in thick brown paper and tied up with string. It was a very exciting parcel, and Jeremy James knew just what was inside it and he wished it was for him and not for Timothy.

Timothy pulled the string apart and tore open the brown paper (which he simply dropped on the floor and left – perhaps as a special treat for his Mummy). Inside was a box, and inside the box was a tank. It was a brown and green tank with a gun that could swivel and fire matches, and it had an engine of its own which meant it could roll along the carpet all by itself, and as it rolled it sparked and made a loud grinding noise, just like a real tank. Jeremy James had seen it working in the shop when he and Mummy had bought it, and he'd seen it again in the living-room when Daddy had tested it (for three-quarters of an hour), and Timothy was very lucky to get a tank

like that because a tank like that was the best present anybody could ever have.

'Oh yes, I've got one like this already,' said Timothy. 'Only the one I've got is bigger.'

A little light of hope shone through Jeremy James's eyes: 'Don't you want it, then?' he said.

'Oh yes, I'll take it,' said Timothy. 'I don't mind having two.'

Out went the little light of hope.

When Timothy had shown off all his presents to all his friends, and had made it clear to them that he had more presents and better presents than they were ever likely to get, and they were very lucky to have a friend like him, all the boys went out into the Smyth-Fortescues' huge garden. There they whooped and warbled, hid and sought, shot and scalped, swung and slid, and machine-gunned one another down until tea-time. Tea was a rich feast of sandwiches, crisps, cakes, jelly, ice-cream and fizzy drinks. Jeremy James's arms, hands and jaws worked almost continuously as he reached, grabbed and chewed, and with all the other little boys doing the same, it wasn't long before the dining-table was as bare as old Mother Hubbard's cupboard.

'Finished, everybody?' asked Mrs Smyth-Fortescue.

'Is there any more?' asked Timothy.

'No, dear.'

'Then I suppose we've finished,' said Timothy, with a glance at the tableful of bare plates.

'Well, I'll just clear the table,' said Mrs Smyth-Fortescue, 'then we can play some nice games, hm?'

While she was clearing the table, Mr Smyth-Fortescue came home from work. He had ginger hair and freckles just like Timothy, and he poked them round the door.

'Are you all enjoying yourselves?' he said.

Nobody took the slightest notice of him, so he went out and wasn't seen again.

'Games now, children!' said Mrs Smyth-Fortescue. 'And there are lovely prizes for the winners.'

'It's bars of chocolate,' said Timothy. 'And I'm going to win them all.'

'I hope I can win one,' said Jeremy James as the prize bars emerged from the sideboard.

'No, you're not allowed,' said Timothy, ''cos it's *my* birthday.'

'Not much fun if we can't win,' said Richard, a fat boy with a round red face.

'I wouldn't win anyway,' said Trevor, a tiny boy who'd already cried twice in the garden.

'Hunt the thimble!' cried Mrs Smyth-Fortescue. 'Everybody leave the room while I hide it!'

And everybody left the room, though Richard and Trevor tried to leave it together, which resulted in a rather squashed Trevor having his third cry of the day.

'Ready!' called Mrs Smyth-Fortescue, and everybody re-entered the room, with Timothy pushing through the door first and Trevor and Jeremy James waiting until it was safe, which meant until Richard had gone in.

'Who's warmest, Mummy?' asked Timothy.

'Jeremy,' said Mrs Smyth-Fortescue.

And as Jeremy James turned round to tell her his name was Jeremy *James*, there was a blur of ginger, and Jeremy James found himself flat on his back next to the piano.

'Got it!' shouted Timothy. 'I got it! Here it is! I got it!'

'Oh well done, dear!' said Mrs Smyth-Fortescue. 'But try not to knock Jeremy down next time.'

Jeremy James rose to his feet and watched Timothy collect his bar of chocolate.

'If he hadn't gone and knocked me over, I'd have had that chocolate,' he said to little Trevor. 'It's not fair.'

'Now we're going to stick the tail on the donkey,' said Mrs Smyth-Fortescue.

'I'll go last,' said Timothy.

'Right, now who's going first?' said Mrs Smyth-Fortescue. 'Come along, Jeremy.'

'Jeremy *James*,' said Jeremy James.

'That's right,' said Mrs Smyth-Fortescue, tying the blindfold over his eyes and spinning him round twice. 'There you are, Jeremy. Now try and put the tail on the donkey.'

There were hoots of laughter as Jeremy James proceeded to stick the tail on the donkey's nose. And the hoots of laughter continued as each boy in turn stabbed the donkey where it shouldn't have been stabbed. Trevor was the nearest – sticking it on the donkey's back leg – until Timothy received the blindfold. He walked straight up to the wall, and without a moment's hesitation stuck the tail in exactly the right position.

'Oh well done, dear!' cried Mrs Smyth-Fortescue, and Timothy collected his second bar of chocolate.

'The blindfold wasn't on properly,' said fat Richard quietly.

'I was winning that,' said little Trevor sadly.

'None of us'll win anything,' said Jeremy James miserably.

And as the afternoon went on, it looked as though he was going to be right. Timothy won all the memory games and all the guessing games, never making a single mistake; and when they played Murder in the Dark, Timothy insisted on being the murderer, which meant there were no prizes anyway because if you knew who the murderer was, there was no game left. Jeremy James wished he could have been the murderer, because he would jolly well have murdered Timothy, and he would *really* have murdered Timothy, and no one would have cried a tear, except perhaps Mrs Smyth-Fortisoup or whatever her name was.

Timothy also won Musical Chairs. He shouldn't have won it, because when he and a boy called Rodney were the last ones left, Timothy sat down *before* the music stopped, but his Mummy *saw* that he'd sat down and *then* she stopped the music. *Everybody* said that was unfair, but Timothy said it was *his* party, and his Mummy said it was his birthday and they should be nice to him and it had been such a lovely party and they shouldn't quarrel, and Timothy said if they didn't let him win they could jolly well go home, and his Mummy said, 'There, there, darling,' and gave him an extra bar of chocolate to comfort him, and then announced that the prize for the last game would be three bars of chocolate, which cheered everybody up.

'I'm going to win it,' said Timothy, which cheered everybody down.

The game was Musical Statues. Mrs Smyth-Fortescue would play the piano, and when she stopped, everybody would stand still, but whoever moved *after* she had stopped would be out. The last one left would be the winner. As she started playing, all the boys started walking, and there were lots of determined faces moving round the room. But with each pause in the music, determination gave way to disappointment and more drooping figures sat down next to the wall. Finally, there were just three boys left: Timothy, Trevor, and Jeremy James (though twice Timothy had moved but he said he hadn't and his Mummy didn't think he had either). Round they went, to the merry tinkle of the piano, and Jeremy James could feel that Timothy was right behind him. He walked faster, but Timothy was still there. He walked slower, and . . . the piano stopped. Bump! Jeremy James went flying, while Timothy, who had walked straight into him, stood as stiff as a candle on a birthday cake.

'Oh bad luck, Jeremy!' called Mrs Smyth-Fortescue.

'It wasn't bad luck,' said Jeremy James, 'he knocked me over.'

'*Very* bad luck,' said Mrs Smyth-Fortescue. 'On we go! I wonder who's going to win!'

'Hmmph!' said Jeremy James, very loud, and slumped down on the floor next to fat Richard. 'It's obvious who's going to win. *He's* going to win. Because *she's* going to let him win.'

'It's a rotten party,' said Richard. 'I wish I hadn't come.'

There were more merry tinkles from the piano, and
then the music stopped. But just as it stopped, Jeremy
James noticed something, and what he noticed was
to make the rotten party into a good party after all.
He noticed that Trevor had stopped quite still on the
far side of the room, and Timothy had stopped quite
still on Jeremy James's side. But whereas Trevor was
standing on the shiny wooden floor, Timothy was
standing on the edge of a round woollen rug. And the
round woollen rug reached just as far as where Jeremy
James was sitting, and the edge of it was a mere inch
away from his right hand. And Jeremy James's right
hand took an immediate decision. It grasped the edge
of the round woollen rug, and gave it a quick, hard
jerk.

'He moved!' cried a dozen voices, and a dozen
fingers pointed as Timothy wobbled, staggered,

almost fell, and then righted himself and pretended nothing had happened.

'I didn't!' said Timothy.

'I'm afraid you did, dear,' said Mrs Smyth-Fortescue.

'We all saw you,' said Jeremy James.

'It wasn't me,' said Timothy, 'it was the floor. The floor moved.'

'No, the floor couldn't have moved, dear,' said Mrs Smyth-Fortescue.

'It did, it did!' said Timothy. 'The floor moved! I felt it! I know what it was! It was the rug!'

Jeremy James frowned.

'Richard pulled the rug!'

Jeremy James stopped frowning.

'It was Richard pulling the rug! It was, Mummy! Ask him! Richard pulled the rug, Mummy!'

'Now then, Richard,' said Mrs Smyth-Fortescue, 'is that true? Did you pull the rug, dear!'

'No I didn't,' said Richard.

'He did!' said Timothy.

'I didn't!' said Richard.

'Jeremy,' said Mrs Smyth-Fortescue, 'did you see Richard pull the rug?'

'No, Mrs Smyth-Fortisook,' said Jeremy James, 'he couldn't have done 'cos I'm sitting right next to him and I'd have seen him. He didn't pull it. Definitely!'

'Very well,' said Mrs Smyth-Fortescue. 'Here you are, Trevor. Come and collect your prize.'

And a dozen voices let out a loud cheer as Trevor collected his three bars of chocolate.

'It's not fair!' wailed Timothy. 'They cheated! It's not fair!'

'Time for everybody to go home now!' said Mrs Smyth-Fortescue.

Timothy stamped his foot, stormed out of the room, up the stairs, and into his bedroom, slamming the door behind him.

Mrs Smyth-Fortescue was taking some of the children home by car, but Jeremy James, Trevor and Richard all lived nearby, so they left together.

'Thank you for the nice party, Mrs Smyth-Forki-suit,' said Jeremy James before they went.

'Glad you enjoyed it, Jeremy,' said Mrs Smyth-Fortescue, giving each of them a balloon and a piece of birthday cake.

'Jeremy *James*,' said Jeremy James.

'That's right,' said Mrs Smyth-Fortescue.

Jeremy James, Trevor and Richard walked together to Jeremy James's front gate. Trevor was loaded down with his balloon, his cake, and his three bars of chocolate, but he had a very important question to ask before they parted company.

'Richard,' he said, '*did* you pull the rug?'

'No,' said Richard, 'I didn't.'

'But I did,' said Jeremy James.

And as they all laughed, Trevor looked at his bars of chocolate, looked at Richard's face, looked at Jeremy James's face, and then looked at his chocolate again.

'Here,' he said. 'I think we *all* deserve a prize.' And he gave each of them a bar of chocolate.

'Was it a nice party, dear?' asked Mummy, opening the door for Jeremy James.

'Yes, thank you,' said Jeremy James. 'I won a bar of chocolate.'

'And what did you win that for?' asked Mummy.

Jeremy James thought for a moment. 'Pulling the rug,' he said.

But that was a game Mummy had never heard of.

Jeremy James and the Tooth-Dragon

Jeremy James had toothache. It was a tooth over on the right-hand side of his mouth, and without a doubt it was his favourite chocolate-crunching, liquorice all-sort-munching tooth. Mummy said it had probably been crunching too much chocolate and too many liquorice all-sorts, and that was why it was hurting, but Jeremy James reckoned it was too many potatoes and too much cabbage that had done the damage. After all, it was his tooth, so he should know what was good and bad for it. But at the moment, he had to confess, the favourite tooth had as little enthusiasm for chocolate and liquorice all-sorts as it had for potatoes and cabbage. It couldn't munch, and it couldn't crunch. All it could do was ache.

'Is it very bad?' asked Mummy at breakfast, as Jeremy James's teeth and tongue wrestled with a cornflake.

Jeremy James pulled a face like a crumpled chocolate wrapper. 'Very, very bad,' he said. Then he remembered something Daddy had said once, when Mummy asked him how he was after he'd mistaken his thumb for the picture-hook. 'It's agony,' said Jeremy James, 'blooming agony.'

'I'll ring Mr Pulham,' said Mummy.

'Who's Mr Pulham?' asked Daddy.

'The dentist!' said Mummy.

'Ah yes,' said Daddy. 'I believe he's of American extraction. What they call a Yank.'

Mummy and Daddy both laughed, but Jeremy James remained very serious, because toothache is no laughing matter.

'Will it hurt?' asked Jeremy James, as he and Mummy pushed the twins along in their pram.

'Not much,' said Mummy.

'How much?' asked Jeremy James.

'Not as much as it's hurting now,' said Mummy. 'And afterwards it'll stop hurting altogether.'

That didn't sound like a lot of hurt, but even a little hurt can be quite painful.

'How do you know how much it's hurting now?' he asked.

'Hmmph!' said Mummy. 'Well, you said it was

blooming agony, so it must be hurting quite a lot. Anyway, you stop worrying about it, and if you're a good boy and you don't cry, I'll give you a nice little bar of chocolate afterwards.'

Jeremy James would have preferred a nice big bar of chocolate, but even a little bar was worth not crying for.

Mr Pulham the dentist was a jolly looking man with a round face, and round spectacles, and a round body which was wrapped up in a long white coat. When the receptionist took Jeremy James into the surgery (leaving Mummy and the twins behind in the waiting room), Mr Pulham was already smiling.

'Hello, Jeremy James,' said Mr Pulham, 'and how are you today?'

'I've got toothache,' said Jeremy James.

'Jolly good,' said Mr Pulham, and gave an even bigger smile.

'He's a little bit deaf,' whispered the receptionist, 'so you'll have to speak louder.'

'I'VE GOT TOOTHACHE!' shouted Jeremy James.

'Ah,' said Mr Pulham, 'then you've come to the right place. You come and sit here, then, Jeremy James.'

Jeremy James sat down in a big black shiny chair, which was surrounded by all sorts of funny-looking machines.

'Hold tight,' said Mr Pulham, and pressed a button. Then Jeremy James suddenly found himself lying down instead of sitting up. Mr Pulham pressed another button, and Jeremy James felt the chair going up in the air.

'GOSH, IT'S LIKE A SPACE ROCKET!' shouted Jeremy James.

'That's right,' said Mr Pulham with a smile. 'For exploring the molar system. Now then, open wide.'

Jeremy James opened his mouth so wide that his face almost disappeared.

'My word,' said Mr Pulham, 'I could almost climb in there and walk around.'

Then he poked and prodded Jeremy James's teeth until he came to the most important one, and this he poked and prodded even more than the others, which proved that it was a very special tooth. It also proved that the dentist knew just where to poke and prod.

'Glug!' said Jeremy James.

'Aha!' said the dentist. 'Oho, mhm, ts, ts.'

Then he straightened up and nodded his head. 'Is that the one, Jeremy James?' he asked.

'Yes,' said Jeremy James. 'I think I've been eating too many potatoes and too much cabbage.'

But the dentist didn't seem to hear, because he turned away and pulled over a long sharp instrument which let out a loud hum.

'Now then,' said Mr Pulham, 'what I'm holding here is a magic sword, called a drill. And inside your tooth is a nasty little dragon whose name is Decay. And that dragon is busy eating your tooth, and that's what's hurting you. So while the dragon's busy eating away, I'm going to creep up on him, and kill him with this magic sword. Only you must keep absolutely still, because if you move, he'll know we're after him and he'll hide away. Right?'

'Right,' said Jeremy James.

'Open up again,' said the dentist. 'And let's catch the dragon in the cave.'

And Jeremy James opened up the cave till his chin nearly tickled his chest. 'Whirr!' went the magic sword, and Jeremy James knew straight away that this was not the sort of magic he liked. It made a nasty noise, had a nasty feel, and gave off a nasty smell.

'Whizz!' went the sword, and Jeremy James tried to think about the bar of chocolate he'd be getting when the dragon was dead.

And then suddenly the sword stopped humming.

'That's it,' said the dentist. 'Killed him dead as a denture. Wash him out now, Jeremy James.'

Jeremy James washed out his mouth and saw little bits and pieces of something disappear down the pan.

'That didn't look much like a dragon,' said Jeremy James.

'What's that?' asked the dentist.

'I SAID HE DIDN'T LOOK MUCH LIKE A DRAGON!' shouted Jeremy James.

'Nor would you if you'd had a fight with my magic sword,' said Mr Pulham. 'Now you lie back again, because we're going to have to fill in the hole the dragon made.'

So Jeremy James lay back while the dentist put some funny-sounding, funny-tasting things in his mouth, and did a little more poking and prodding and scraping. Jeremy James thought about his bar of chocolate again, and decided that this was the easiest way of getting chocolate that he'd ever come across. All he had to do was lie still with his mouth open. And he reckoned he could lie still with his mouth open all day long if necessary. If Mummy were to offer him a really giant bar of chocolate, he could even break the world record for lying still with his mouth open.

'Good lad,' said the dentist, taking all the funny things out of Jeremy James's mouth. 'Rinse it out again.'

The dentist went with Jeremy James to the waiting-room, where Mummy sat holding Christopher in one arm and Jennifer in the other. She was joggling them up and down, and Jennifer was giggling, and Christopher was scowling.

'All done,' said Mr Pulham. 'Best patient I've had all day. He's as bright as a gold filling, aren't you, Jeremy James?'

'Well, it was quite easy,' said Jeremy James. 'I just thought about my bar of chocolate.'

'What's that?' said the dentist. 'Now then, nothing

51

to eat for two hours, and stay off the sweeties, Jeremy James, eh? Dragons always like sweet things, and you don't want any more dragons in there, do you?'

'Well, no-o, but . . .' Jeremy James didn't finish his sentence, because he wasn't quite sure what he wanted to say, and even if he had been, the dentist probably wouldn't have heard anyway.

'Mummy,' said Jeremy James, as he and Mummy pushed the twins homewards in the pram, 'will I have a bar of chocolate every time I go to the dentist's?'

'I shouldn't think so,' said Mummy. 'You heard what the dentist said – chocolate's bad for your teeth.'

'But if I *do* get another dragon in there, will you give me a bar of chocolate for not crying?'

'Maybe,' said Mummy – which was another typical Mummy reply. 'Let's hope you won't get any more dragons, though. You don't want any more of that blooming agony, do you?'

And Jeremy James had to admit that he would prefer to do without the blooming agony. But on the other hand, lying still with your mouth open was such a nice way of earning chocolate, and if you had to have a dragon before you could not-cry at the dentist's well . . . hmmph . . .

'Maybe,' said Jeremy James. 'We'll see.'

The strike

Mummy, Jeremy James and the twins were out for a walk. The twins sat cushioned in their pram like a prince and princess in their carriage, Jeremy James pretended he was a racing driver and pushed them as fast as he could, and Mummy occasionally steered or braked when silly pedestrians got in the way. Of course Mummy didn't know that Jeremy James was the world champion driver who could *deliberately* miss toddlers, old men and fat ladies by a couple of inches when he wanted to – otherwise she would never have interfered.

They had almost reached the park when they heard the distant oompah-oompah of a brass band, and as Jeremy James wanted to see the soldiers, they walked on in the direction of the sound. However, there were no soldiers at all, but a band and a large crowd of ordinary men and women carrying banners and shouting things like: 'We want more!' and 'We want it now!' and 'Up with our wages!' and 'Down with the Government!' Mummy explained to Jeremy James that these were workers, and they were on strike. Jeremy James wanted to know what 'on strike' meant, and Mummy explained that it meant not working. Then Jeremy James wanted to know how you could be a worker and not work, and Mummy said that was a very good question.

One of the workers who wasn't working got up on

a box and shouted out 'Brothers!' till everyone was quiet. Jeremy James frowned in disbelief.

'They can't all be his brothers!' he said to Mummy. 'They'd never be able to get into the house.'

'They're not his real brothers,' said Mummy. 'It's just a way of talking.'

Jeremy James thought it was a silly way of talking, but as these were workers who didn't work, it was hardly surprising that they were also brothers who weren't brothers. Jeremy James wondered if the women were sisters who weren't sisters.

'Brothers,' said the man on the box, 'we need more money, we deserve more money, and we shall get more money!'

Everybody cheered, and Jeremy James cheered too, because he felt exactly the same way about his money. The man on the box went on to say that he was getting the same money as somebody else, but he should be getting more. Then a moment later he said somebody else was getting more money than he was, and that wasn't fair. And after that he said he didn't want more money than other people but he and other people should all have more money than everybody else, and nobody should have less than other people but everybody should get more and then it would be fair. Jeremy James found it all rather hard to follow, but he cheered all the same because he was sure the man on the box was on his side.

On the way home, Jeremy James asked Mummy quite a lot of questions. For instance, he wanted to know just how the non-working workers would get the more money which they deserved. Mummy said that by not working, they hoped to force the people with the money to give them more. Jeremy James thought this meant that the less you worked, the more money you would get, but Mummy said it was all very complicated, and so Jeremy James reckoned it was just another way of talking, like the unworkers and the unbrothers.

'Why doesn't Daddy go on strike?' asked Jeremy James. 'Then he could get more money, too.'

'If Daddy went on strike,' said Mummy, 'nobody would notice any difference.'

That was also pretty hard for Jeremy James to understand. It seemed to him that there would be a big difference between Daddy locked away in his study, and Daddy sitting on the carpet playing trains and soldiers and cowboys. But grown-ups have their own ways of talking and thinking, and Jeremy James could only shake his head and wonder if, when he grew up, he would think as grown-ups do.

At tea, Jeremy James sprang a little surprise on Mummy and Daddy. Mummy asked him to go and fetch a pot of jam.

'No,' said Jeremy James.

'Pardon?' said Mummy.

'I'm on strike,' said Jeremy James.

Mummy and Daddy looked at each other.

'This is very sudden,' said Daddy. 'You might have given us a warning.'

'I only just decided,' said Jeremy James. 'I think I deserve more money.'

'Aha,' said Daddy, 'don't we all!'

'And I'm not going to do any more work,' said Jeremy James, 'until my wages go up.'

'You'd better get that jam yourself, dear,' said

Daddy to Mummy, 'we've got an industrial crisis on our hands. Now then, Jeremy James, what sort of wages were you thinking of?'

'A hundred pounds a week,' said Jeremy James. 'A hundred pounds and . . . fourpence.'

'*And* fourpence,' said Daddy. 'Phew, that's pretty steep, with that fourpence.'

'Well I think I deserve it,' said Jeremy James. 'And other people shouldn't get more . . . less . . . more than me.'

'You mean,' said Mummy, 'you're not going to do any more work at all?'

'No,' said Jeremy James, 'except I might go outside and wave a flag and talk.'

'Who to?' asked Daddy.

'Some of the brothers,' said Jeremy James. 'You know, the brothers who aren't brothers.'

'Ah!' said Daddy. '*Those* brothers.'

When tea was finished, Mummy and Daddy cleared the table, and Jeremy James went and sat in the armchair. Mummy and Daddy knew it was no use asking him to help, because people on strike don't help anyone – they just unwork until they get their money. He could hear them talking and laughing in the kitchen as they washed the dishes, and he smiled to himself because with a hundred pounds and fourpence he could buy tons and tons of chocolate and toys and sweets as well as a tricycle with a bell *and* a saddlebag, and all he had to do for the money was nothing – just hours and hours of nothing. Life couldn't be simpler.

At bedtime, Jeremy James kissed Mummy and Daddy goodnight, and – as they hadn't made any further mention of his strike or his money – he asked them when he would be getting his hundred pounds and fourpence.

'Can't tell you yet,' said Daddy. 'There'll have to be negotiations and committees of inquiry first, and we may even have to go to arbitration . . .'

Daddy always liked to make up long words when he didn't want to answer questions. Mummy just said: 'Hmmph' and 'We'll see' and 'Goodnight, dear.'

As he lay in bed, Jeremy James wondered whether perhaps he shouldn't have asked for a bit more money. A hundred pounds and fourpence had seemed a lot at the time, but there must be people who got even more than that, and the man on the box had certainly said it wasn't fair if *anybody* got more than . . . or was it less than . . . anybody else. However, Jeremy James decided that if a hundred pounds and fourpence wasn't enough, he could always go on strike again later.

The next morning, Mummy sprang a little surprise on Jeremy James. There was no breakfast.

'No breakfast?' said Jeremy James.

'I'm on strike,' said Mummy. 'Sorry, you'll have to go without.'

Sitting at the table was Daddy, and sitting in front of Daddy was a slippery fried egg and a crisp slice of bacon.

'No use looking at mine,' said Daddy. 'You'll have to get your own.'

'But I can't cook egg and bacon,' said Jeremy James.

'Awful, isn't it?' said Daddy. 'Let's hope Mummy's strike won't last too long.'

'Couldn't you cook it for me?' asked Jeremy James.

'Sorry,' said Daddy, 'I'm on strike, too.'

Jeremy James frowned. After all, if *everybody* went on strike, who was going to do the work?

'Well, what should I have for my breakfast?' he said.

'Don't ask me,' said Mummy.

'That's up to you,' said Daddy. 'You can help yourself to a glass of water, can't you?'

For breakfast, Jeremy James had a glass of water, and a very dry crust of bread which he found at the bottom of an otherwise empty bread-bin. It wasn't a very nice breakfast.

After the not-very-nice breakfast, Jeremy James waited to be told to go and do his Number Two. He had been looking forward to saying 'No, I'm on strike', but Mummy and Daddy did not seem in the least bit interested. Mummy was reading a magazine, and Daddy was reading the paper, and hours and hours went by.

'Aren't you going to tell me to do my Number Two?' said Jeremy James.

'Of course not,' said Mummy. 'We're on strike.'

That was certainly not the conversation Jeremy James had looked forward to. Slowly, and rather miserably, he made his way upstairs. When he had not done his Number Two, and had not washed his face and not brushed his teeth, he looked round for his clothes. His dirty clothes were still where he had left them last night, but there were no clean clothes anywhere.

'Mummy,' called Jeremy James, 'I can't find any clean clothes.'

'I don't suppose there are any,' called Mummy. 'You'll have to wear your dirty ones.'

'But they're all muddy and horrible,' called Jeremy James.

'You'd better wash them out, then,' called Mummy. 'I'm on strike.'

Jeremy James went downstairs again.

'Still in your pyjamas?' said Daddy.

'You do look miserable,' said Mummy. 'What's the matter?'

'I didn't know *you* were going on strike,' said Jeremy James. 'I thought it was just going to be me.'

'Well, you gave us an idea,' said Mummy. 'And it does make life easier when you don't have to work, doesn't it?'

'When is your strike going to finish?' asked Jeremy James.

'When I get what I want,' said Mummy.

'What's that?' asked Jeremy James.

'I thought I'd ask for the same as you,' said Mummy. 'One hundred pounds and fourpence. We should both get the same, otherwise it wouldn't be fair.'

Jeremy James saw a glimmer of hope: 'Is Daddy going to give it to you?' he asked.

'No, *you* have to give it to me,' said Mummy. 'I'm only not working for you. I'm still working for Daddy and the twins.'

'But . . .' said Jeremy James, 'I haven't got a hundred pounds and fourpence.'

'Ah,' said Daddy, 'now I've had an idea about that. Supposing, Jeremy James, you were to end your strike, but instead of paying you your one hundred pounds and fourpence I gave it to Mummy instead, then it would be just like you paying Mummy, and so she could end her strike as well. How does that . . . um . . . strike you?'

Jeremy James thought about it, and the more he thought about it, the better it seemed.

'Will I be able to have my breakfast, then?' he asked.

'Of course,' said Daddy. 'That's part of the agreement.'

'And clean clothes?' said Jeremy James.

'So long as you agree to the terms,' said Daddy. Jeremy James gave a smile as wide as a rasher of bacon, and his eyes shone as brightly as a newly fried egg.

'Yes, please,' he said.

'There you are,' said Daddy, 'all that's needed is goodwill and good sense on both sides, and industrial relations are simple as ABC.'

Jeremy James wasn't quite sure what 'industrial relations' were, but he did know that breakfast that day tasted nicer than it had ever tasted before.

The hunt

It was a typical English summer's day, with the rain slanting down from a blueless grey sky, and Jeremy James was bored. Mummy was resting on the settee, the twins were asleep upstairs (the twins seemed to have a funny effect on Mummy: whenever they went to sleep, she tried to go to sleep, too) – and Daddy was in his study, playing with his typewriter. Jeremy James sat on the living-room floor, surrounded by picture-books, toy soldiers, and his train set, and he didn't know what to do. He'd read all the picture-books, he'd killed all the soldiers, and he'd called his train set out on strike. It was a hundred years till teatime, and a hundred years since lunch, and Mummy shouldn't have curled up on the settee – she should have taken Jeremy James somewhere nice, or played a game with him, or left him a mountain of chocolate to eat through.

'Ts!' said Jeremy James nice and loud, and watched Mummy's eyes in the hope that they might flicker open, but Mummy's eyes remained firmly closed. 'Hmmph!' he said, but still there was no attention.

'If I was Christopher or Jennifer,' thought Jeremy James, 'I could open my mouth and howl, and then Mummy would jump up and hug me and ask me what's the matter. But if I open my Jeremy James mouth and howl, all I shall get is a telling-off.'

Jeremy James gave a loud sigh, but still Mummy's eyes stayed shut.

Jeremy James would certainly have rolled over and died of boredom if, at that moment, there hadn't been a sudden dramatic event. The room was entered by a loud buzz. And in the middle of the buzz, carrying it all over the living-room, was a nasty, bad-tempered, thoroughly dangerous wasp. It zoomed over Jeremy James's head, battered at the window like a shower of hailstones, and then came humming back across the room, right past Mummy and on to the arm of the settee. Surely Mummy would wake up now, with all that noise. But no, Mummy had heard nothing, and she couldn't know that just a few inches away from her leg crawled a yellow and black striped monster that might attack her at any minute. Perhaps he should wake her up to warn her. But would she be pleased or not? Jeremy James could imagine her saying: 'Oh thank you, Jeremy James, you've saved my life, what a good boy you are, here's a whole bar of chocolate!' But he could also imagine her saying 'Ts!' or 'Hmmph!' and 'Fancy waking me up for that!' It was a difficult decision to take, but he didn't have to take it because abruptly the wasp took off again and made a wasp-line for the window. And there it stayed, crawling up and down the glass, no doubt pleased to be out of the pouring rain.

Jeremy James tiptoed across the room and stood near, but not too near the window. The wasp didn't look quite so dangerous when it wasn't flying. In fact, it looked rather silly. It was waggling its black feelers up and down, and its little wings were as thin as tracing paper, and the yellow and black bit hardly seemed to belong to the wasp at all – it was just being dragged along behind, like Jeremy James when he went shopping with Mummy. Jeremy James decided that without its buzz, the wasp was a bit of a disappointment. He took one step nearer the window, stretched out his arm, stretched out one finger, and BUZZ! went the wasp, and whined straight past Jeremy James's left ear, so close that he even felt the draught. Jeremy James jumped back, and his heart was going thumpety-thump. Wasps *were* dangerous. And this wasp was particularly dangerous, because it was the sort of wasp that made you think it was silly but then suddenly leapt out at you when you weren't expecting it. Jeremy James reckoned a wasp like that could do a lot of damage if it was allowed to go on tricking people, and the person who managed to rid the world of such a dangerous animal would be a real hero, worthy of a hundred bars of chocolate.

The wasp continued to whizz from one side of the room to the other. It would take a lot of catching, a wasp that could whizz like that, but on the other hand, wouldn't Mummy and Daddy be pleased when he showed them its dead body! Especially when they knew what a *dangerous* wasp it had been. Now what could he use to kill it with? Mummy usually trod on insects she wanted to kill, but you couldn't tread on an insect that was whizzing round the room. The wasp hurtled past Jeremy James's right ear, and Jeremy James almost fell over as he got out of the way. This wasp was really looking for trouble, and it was going to be a question of who caught whom first. Jeremy James had an idea. He couldn't lift his leg up that high, but he could certainly lift his arm, and if he put his slipper on the end of his arm, well, the wasp wouldn't know the difference.

Jeremy James stood in the middle of the room, slipper in hand, and waited. Zoom came the wasp, swish went the slipper, but the wasp was already a mile away. It was not going to be easy. Jeremy James tried a few random swishes, in the hope that the wasp might accidentally bump into the slipper, but his arm soon got tired and the wasp didn't have any accidents, so Jeremy James stopped swishing. Then Jeremy James lost sight and sound of the wasp. The room was completely silent, save for the gentle rise and fall of Mummy sleeping. Where was the enemy? Jeremy James stood quite still, eyes jerking as he scanned the ceiling, walls, floor and furniture. Had it gone? Was it hiding? Was it fast asleep somewhere? *Did* wasps go to sleep?

Jeremy James didn't like the silence. The wasp's buzz was nasty, but its silence was nastier. For all he knew, the wasp might be sitting just a couple of inches away, watching him and planning to sting him just when he wasn't looking. At least when it was whizzing around, you knew where it was, but if you didn't know where it was, it could be *anywhere*. It could even be on Jeremy James himself! Jeremy James had a quick look down at his body and legs. Then he twisted round to look at the back of his legs. No wasp. He humped his shoulders up and down. No buzz. All the same, he didn't feel very safe. Very slowly and carefully, he padded round the room, slipper held high and eyes darting from side to side.

The wasp was not on the window. The wasp was

not on the settee. The wasp was not on Mummy. The wasp was not on either armchair. The wasp was not on the sideboard. The wasp was not . . . but it *was* . . . it was there, on the mantelpiece. To be precise, it was on the vase of flowers on the mantelpiece, waggling its feelers and ducking its silly black head. And it hadn't seen Jeremy James. It had no idea that it had been spotted, and it had no idea that Jeremy James was now creeping up behind it, slipper raised and heart pounding. Jeremy James padded closer and closer, an inch at a time, until he could actually see the wasp's black eyes and yellow cheeks, and its striped shopping-bag quivering a little behind it. This was the most dangerous wasp that ever lived, and the safety of the world depended now on Jeremy James and his slipper. The great hunter paused, gathered all his strength together, and then in one swift movement brought his mighty weapon down on the back of his deadly enemy . . .

What happened next came as a terrible shock to Jeremy James, to his Mummy, and above all to the wasp. There was a shattering crash as the vase came tumbling down from the mantelpiece and smashed to bits on the hearth below. In no time there were flowers and pools of water all over the living-room carpet, and Mummy had leapt off the settee with a face as white as a snowdrop.

'What was that?' she said. 'What on earth was that?'

And then she saw what on earth it was, and she saw Jeremy James standing over the bits of vase and the mess of flowers and the puddles of water, and he was holding a slipper in his hand, and he was looking up at her with eyes that were very round and rather frightened.

Before she could say a word, Daddy came bounding in.

'What on earth was that?' he said. 'I thought I heard a . . . Good Lord!'

And Daddy also saw the jumble of china and petals and leaves and soggy carpet.

'It's our best vase!' said Mummy.

'Well, it was,' said Daddy.

Mummy hurried out and came back carrying a cloth and a brush and a pan.

'What happened?' asked Daddy.

'There was a wasp,' said Jeremy James. 'It was a great big dangerous one.'

'And this great big dangerous wasp took a dislike

to Mummy's vase,' said Daddy, 'and pushed it off the mantelpiece.'

'No,' said Jeremy James. 'I was trying to kill it.'

'I see,' said Daddy. 'But instead of killing the wasp, you killed the vase.'

'Well,' said Jeremy James, 'the wasp was sitting on the vase.'

'Aha,' said Daddy, 'so you hit the wasp *and* the vase.'

'Well, I'm not sure if I hit the wasp,' said Jeremy James.

'But we can be fairly sure that you hit the vase,' said Daddy.

'Yes,' said Jeremy James.

Mummy held up a tiny limp yellow and black thing. 'Is this your great big dangerous wasp?' she asked.

Jeremy James got down on his hands and knees and looked very closely. 'Yes,' he said, 'it is! That's the one! 'Cos it had those stripes!'

Daddy nodded thoughtfully. 'Not a bad shot, then,' he said.

'All the same,' said Mummy, 'in future, Jeremy James, leave the wasps alone.' Then she looked at Daddy. 'Vase today, window tomorrow.'

Daddy grinned. 'Lucky for you it didn't land on your nose,' he said.

'Oh I wouldn't have killed it if it had been on Mummy's nose,' said Jeremy James. 'Because that would have woken Mummy up.'

Pancakes and blackberries

It was one of those warm, gentle September Saturdays which Daddy said were perfect for watching football and Mummy said were perfect for a family outing. Daddy wondered whether perhaps the family would like to go on an outing to a football match, but Mummy said she wouldn't, and Jeremy James said he'd prefer a place that sold strawberries and cream, and the twins said gurgle and glug, which meant they would go where they were taken. And so they were taken blackberry picking.

Daddy drove the whole family out into the country in their newly patched new car, and as they went down the narrow lanes, Mummy looked at the hedges on one side and Jeremy James looked at those on the other, and Daddy tried to look at the hedges on both sides and the road in the middle. Sometimes when Daddy was looking at a hedge on one side, Mummy would take a look at the road in the middle and would shout out 'Watch it!' and Daddy would suddenly swing the steering-wheel and say 'OK. Don't panic!' and Jeremy James would say 'There's some blackberries!' and Daddy would say 'Where!' and Mummy would say 'Keep your eye on the road!' and Daddy would swing the steering-wheel again. Blackberry picking was quite exciting, really.

At last, Daddy pulled up on a broad grass verge at the side of the road, and they all got out. Mummy

put the twins in the pram, and Daddy fetched the baskets and sticks from the back of the car (the sticks were for pulling down brambles that were out of reach). All along the side of the road, the hedges were full of ripe berries, but what had attracted Jeremy James's attention was a tree-lined path just behind where Daddy had stopped the car. It was a very interesting path, because you couldn't see where it led to.

'Can I go and pick blackberries down there?' asked Jeremy James, and Mummy nodded so off he went.

'Don't go too far away!' called Mummy.

Jeremy James wondered how far away too far away would be, but he just called out: 'I won't!' and carried on running.

There were no blackberries at all along the tree-lined path, but as there was a bend in the path, Jeremy James trotted on because – as Mummy kept saying to Daddy when Daddy took his eyes off the road – you never know what's round the bend. Round the bend, in fact, there were more trees and more bends, but still no blackberries. The only exciting thing along this path was the huge collection of what Daddy had once called 'pancakes'. 'Pancakes' were cows' Number Two, and a lot of cows had been along this path. Jeremy James quite enjoyed leaping over or swerving round the pancakes, because they were all very dangerous – even the old dried ones. If your foot just touched a tiny piece, there was certain to be a terrible explosion, and the whole world would go up in flames. You had to be very strong and very brave and very clever to avoid dangerous pancakes like these.

At last the tree-lined, pancake-carpeted path came to an end, and Jeremy James found himself in front of a high wooden gate which led into a huge green field. And on both sides of the gate, and all round the huge green field, there were thousands and thousands of blackberry bushes covered in millions and millions of blackberries. The blackberries outside the field were big and juicy, but the blackberries inside the field were even bigger and even juicier, and those – Jeremy James knew straight away – were without doubt the best blackberries in the world. Jeremy James reached through the bars of the gate and picked a berry. He popped it into his mouth. It was the sweetest, yummiest berry he had ever tasted. A second berry merely confirmed the impression made by the first, and a third berry merely confirmed the impression made by the second. Jeremy James could already taste the fruits of his labour as he squeezed through the wooden bars and into the green field.

What he had not noticed from outside – because they had been hidden from view by the thick brambles – was a herd of cows in the green field. Most of them were on the far side, but there were a few fairly close, peacefully chewing the grass and swishing their tails from side to side. Jeremy James did not have a very high opinion of cows. They always moved so slowly, and they just chewed and stared and did their Number Two all over the place, and they said nothing but moo . . . cows were boring animals. You never saw cows at the zoo, because they just weren't interesting enough. You saw elephants at the zoo, because they were huge and tough and could whiffle things up with their noses. And you saw lions and tigers, because they could run fast and could roar. And you saw snakes and wolves and crocodiles, because they were deadly and frightening and interesting. You never saw boring old cows. Jeremy James shouted 'Moo!' at the cow that was nearest to him, but it just stood and blinked and went on chewing. The only dangerous thing about cows was their pancakes, but even they weren't interesting – just soft and smelly, like the twins' nappies. 'Moo!' said Jeremy James again, and stepped carefully towards the brambles.

The blackberries hung in glossy clusters from the bushes, and Jeremy James found it very hard to keep his eating up with his picking. But the most difficult part was avoiding the thorns. If you got pricked with one of those, you would go to sleep for a hundred years, and so you had to be very strong and very brave and very clever to keep your fingers away from them. Only a world champion picker could do it.

There were at least a dozen blackberries in Jeremy James's basket, and at least three dozen in his tummy, when he decided to have a rest. Blackberry picking is quite hard on the arms, let alone on the jaws, and so he turned round to talk with the cows. Some of them had come closer now, and there was one that was standing right in the middle of the field and was actually looking in Jeremy James's direction.

'Moo moo!' cried Jeremy James, but the cow neither mooed nor moved; it just stood there and stared.

'Cows are boring!' cried Jeremy James. 'Moo moo!'

The cow stood as still as a bottle of milk.

'You're too stupid even to be in a zoo!' cried Jeremy James. 'Moo moo! Zoo zoo!'

The cow suddenly lowered its head slightly and made a funny movement with its foot, as if wiping it on the grass.

'It stepped into a pancake!' giggled Jeremy James. 'Moo moo! Poo poo!'

The cow stopped wiping its foot, and took a few steps towards Jeremy James. Jeremy James stopped shouting poo poo and watched the cow. The cow watched Jeremy James.

'She knows what I'm saying,' thought Jeremy James. 'I can really speak cow language!' He took a deep breath, puffed out his chest till it was as round as a pancake, and let out the loudest moo ever to pass the lips of an uncow moo-speaker.

This seemed to have an extraordinary effect on the cow in the middle of the field, for it suddenly lowered its head almost to the ground, and began running at full speed straight towards Jeremy James. For a quarter of a second, Jeremy James stood watching the running cow, and in that quarter of a second a voice in his head told him that even if cows couldn't run, this one jolly well could, and if he didn't want to end up as a blackberry pancake, he had better start running too. Jeremy James dropped his basket and his stick, and dashed towards the gate. Behind him, he could hear loud thumps and a noise like a speeded-up Daddy's snore. He dived headfirst under the lowest wooden bar and scrambled out on to the path. Then without even stopping to look behind him, he raced away with legs whirling like propellers, and they carried him at world record speed over the pancakes, past the trees, round the bends, on to the grass verge, and into Daddy's arms.

'Ouf!' said Daddy. 'And where are you running to?'

'It's a cow!' said Jeremy James, with a puff and a pant. 'A great big cow!'

'Cows won't hurt you,' said Daddy.

'This one will,' said Jeremy James. 'I said something it didn't like, and it ran after me. If I hadn't dived under the gate, it would have gobbled me up!'

'What did you say to it?' asked Daddy.

'Moo,' said Jeremy James.

'That sounds a reasonable thing to say to a cow,' said Daddy. 'Where's your basket?'

'I left it there,' said Jeremy James. 'And my stick. I dropped them when the cow ran after me.'

'Jeremy James,' said Mummy, 'cows don't run after people.'

'This one did,' said Jeremy James.

'Come on, let's go and get your basket,' said Daddy.

Daddy took Jeremy James's hand, and they walked back up the path together.

'Now where is it?' asked Daddy.

'In the field,' said Jeremy James.

Daddy looked over the brambles at the cows quietly chewing the grass. 'Wait here, then,' he said, and climbed up the gate. He had just put his leg over the top when a great big cow raised its head and looked at him. Daddy looked back at the cow. Then Daddy looked a little more closely at the cow. And then Daddy brought his leg back, and climbed down the gate again.

'Aren't you going to get it?' asked Jeremy James.

'No,' said Daddy. Then he picked Jeremy James up in his arms and lifted him high. 'You see that nice cow over there,' he said. 'Well, it's got an udder underneath – like a glove turning into a balloon. But that not-so-nice cow over there hasn't got an udder. And do you know why? It's because he's not a cow at all – he's a bull. And if you ever see a bull in a field, Jeremy James, keep out. Right?'

Daddy humped Jeremy James over his shoulder and set off back down the path. Jeremy James raised his head to have a last look at the cow without an udder.

'Moo moo zoo zoo,' he murmured.

'What did you say to him?' asked Daddy.

'I told him he ought to be in a zoo,' said Jeremy James.

'And what did he say to that?' asked Daddy.

'I don't think he heard,' replied Jeremy James. 'I only said it quietly.'

Jeremy James and the ghost

It was a wild and stormy night. The thunder rumbled like the tummy of a hungry giant, the wind howled like fifty pairs of twins, and the rain rattled at the window like Daddy's typewriter in between pauses. From time to time Jeremy James's bedroom was lit by lightning, revealing Jeremy James himself sitting up in bed, wide-eyed, knees bent, shoulders hunched, with the blankets tightly wrapped around him.

Crash thump rumble rumble, went the thunder, and the curtains blew high into the room, whirling and flapping like ghosts chained to the wall. Jeremy James knew that they were curtains, and he knew that curtains are curtains and ghosts are ghosts, but he couldn't help wondering whether perhaps ghosts might *disguise* themselves as curtains, and whether perhaps these particular curtains might not be the ideal sort of curtains for ghosts to disguise themselves as.

Bang, bump, grumble grumble, went the thunder, and Jeremy James wished he hadn't watched 'The Haunted House' on television that evening. Mummy had said he shouldn't because it would give him bad dreams, but Jeremy James had said he never had bad dreams, and Daddy had said he was a big boy now so maybe just this once . . . but Jeremy James didn't feel like a big boy now, and he was having very nasty dreams even though he wasn't asleep. All those

creaking doors and dark shadows and floating figures and loud screams and whispering voices and wild stormy nights just like this one . . . What was that?

Jeremy James sat even more up than he had been sitting before.

Creak, said the floorboards outside his bedroom door.

Crack, boom, mumble mumble, went the thunder, and ratatat went the rain, and howl went the wind – but definitely creak went the floorboards. And then click went the door-handle. And squeak-creak went the door. Jeremy James felt himself go all cold, and his body went as stiff as a block of ice, and he rolled his eyes sideways to try and see what was happening, because he couldn't even turn his head, which had somehow got locked onto his shoulders. In the darkness he could just make out the dim shape of the door as it slowly swung open. And into the room floated a figure in a long robe that glowed with an eerie light. There was a flash that illuminated the whole room for a second, and Jeremy James froze into an even stiffer block of ice as he saw the face of the ghost: it was a skull! He saw the white cheeks and the hollow shadows of the eyes, and on top of the skull he saw a kind of crown – but then everything was dark again, and Jeremy James wished the floor would open up so that he could drop down into the living-room and be safe. It was no use calling out for Mummy or Daddy, because the ghost would hear, and the ghost was nearer to him than Mummy and Daddy. It would get him long before they could come. Maybe the ghost hadn't seen him. He could still hide.

Slowly, very slowly Jeremy James eased himself

down the bed, covering his tummy, then his chest, then his arms . . . Where was it? Ah, there it was, right at the foot of the bed. Was it going past the bed? Yes, it was moving, slowly, silently, away towards the window. Jeremy James could see the curtain-ghosts reaching out towards the new ghost, and a little beam of warm hope shone into his frozen brain: perhaps the ghost didn't even know about Jeremy James; perhaps it only knew about the curtain-ghosts. It had only come to join the others.

The ghost went all the way to the window, and Jeremy James turned his head to watch, and he must have turned his body a little as well because kerdoing went the bed-springs and then swish went the curtain-ghosts, and split, roll, hmmph hmmph, went the thunder, and . . . 'Are you awake, Jeremy James?' came a strange, cold, whispering voice.

'N . . . n . . . no,' said Jeremy James. 'I'm as . . . s . . . sleep.'

But the ghost didn't believe him. And as another flash of lightning lit up the crowned skull and the shiny robe, Jeremy James saw the ghost floating away from the window and towards his bed.

'Yarrk!' gulped Jeremy James, and pulled the covers right over his head. So long as he couldn't see the ghost, he reckoned, the ghost couldn't see him. But the ghost began to tug at the covers, and he could hear its whispery voice and feel its clammy fingers . . . but he held on tight, keeping the blankets over his face and his ears, and rolling his body into a little ball like a hedgehog without any spikes.

The ghost whispered and tugged for a little while longer, but then seemed to give up. Jeremy James

could hear and feel nothing there at all. Then . . .
Clatter! That wasn't the wind or the rain or the
thunder. It sounded as if it came from the window.
Jeremy James wanted to look, but didn't dare. He
just held on tight and listened. Nothing. Wait! A
squeaky creak . . . then a click. That must be the door.
Had the ghost gone? Or was it a trick just to make
him come out? You never know with ghosts – one
moment they're gone and the next they're with you
again. Or clattering the window or pulling at your
cover. Jeremy James stayed quite still in his safe
hiding-place. He counted all the way up to twenty,
and then up to ten again just to make quite sure.
Then he slowly loosened his grip on the blankets –
not completely, because he had to be ready to pull
them tight if the ghost attacked again, but just enough
to make the ghost think he was relaxing. Nothing
happened. Still safe. Jeremy James very, very slowly
lifted the blankets, and very, very, very slowly poked
his whole head out from underneath. And still nothing
happened.

Now, even less slowly, and in fact quite quickly,
Jeremy James poked an arm out from under the covers
and reached for the light switch at the side of the bed.
He'd been told it was to be used in emergencies, like
wanting to do a wee in the middle of the night. This
was certainly more important than doing a wee in the
night. On went the light. There was no ghost. And
the door was closed. He looked round the room till
his gaze rested on the window. The curtains – they
were still! So the curtain-ghosts had gone, too! That
must be it: the ghost had come to collect his friends,
and they'd all gone out together. And if Jeremy James

hadn't had the presence of mind to dive beneath the blankets and fight them off, they would have taken him with them.

Jeremy James sat up in bed and felt very pleased with himself. There can't be many little boys, he thought, who have fought off a ghost and lived to tell the tale. Perhaps there would be a film about it tomorrow on the television. He would have liked to go and tell Mummy and Daddy about it straight away, but perhaps if he opened the bedroom door . . . well, you never knew what you might find out on the landing. He'd tell them tomorrow.

Plunk, pop, mm mm, went the thunder, which suddenly seemed quite a long way away. And the wind seemed only to be whimpering, and the rain to be lightly pattering. The night wasn't at all frightening really. You just need a little bit of courage, and even ghosts will leave you alone. Jeremy James smiled to himself, pinned an imaginary medal to his chest, and suddenly felt rather sleepy. He put out the light, curled up into a little ball, and – just to make quite sure of things – pulled the covers up over his head.

'I saw a ghost last night,' said Jeremy James at breakfast.

'Did you, dear?' said Mummy, presenting him with down-to-earth bacon and eggs. 'That must have been nice.'

'No, it wasn't,' said Jeremy James. 'It was a bit frightening. Well, it would have been frightening if I'd been frightened.'

'But you weren't frightened, eh?' said Daddy over the top of the newspaper.

'No,' said Jeremy James.

'Good for you,' said Daddy.

'It had a long white robe on, and a crown, and its face was a skull,' said Jeremy James, 'and it knew my name, 'cos it spoke to me in a horrible whispery voice.'

'When was this, dear?' said Mummy.

'Last night,' said Jeremy James. 'During the storm. It came into my room and tried to take me away.'

'What did you say it looked like?' said Daddy.

'It had a crown on,' said Jeremy James, 'and its face was a skull, and it was wearing a shiny robe.'

Daddy's face suddenly broke into a big grin. And when Jeremy James looked at Mummy, she was grinning, too.

'It wasn't funny,' said Jeremy James. 'I could have been killed!'

But then they started laughing, and they went on laughing until they just couldn't laugh any more.

'That ghost,' said Daddy, puffing and wiping his eyes, 'do you know who it was, Jeremy James?'

'It was a dead king,' said Jeremy James. 'That's who it was.'

'It was me,' said Mummy, 'in my nightdress. I had white cream over my face, and I was wearing curlers. I always put them in before I go to bed!'

'Mummy came in to close your window,' said Daddy. 'Because of the storm.'

And Jeremy James just sat there while Mummy and Daddy laughed out their last reserves of laughter. And then they stopped laughing, and Mummy gave Jeremy James a big hug.

'But weren't you brave!' she said. 'You were so

brave that it never occurred to me you might be frightened.'

'I wasn't frightened,' said Jeremy James.

'That's what I mean,' said Mummy. 'You *are* a brave boy.'

'Well, I can tell you,' said Daddy, 'when I see Mummy in face-cream and curlers, it frightens *me*.'

And as a special reward for his extraordinary bravery, Jeremy James was given a shiny 10p piece, and permission to spend it on a bar of chocolate. Which only goes to show that even if parents do the strangest things most of the time, they do just occasionally have some connection with the real world.

Father Christmas and Father Christmas

Jeremy James first met Father Christmas one Saturday morning in a big shop. He was a little surprised to see him there, because it was soon going to be Christmas, and Jeremy James thought Santa Claus really ought to be somewhere in the North Pole filling sacks with presents and feeding his reindeer. However, there he was, on a platform in the toy department, handing out little parcels to the boys and girls who came to see him.

'Here you are, Jeremy James,' said Daddy, and handed him a 50p piece.

'What's that for?' asked Jeremy James.

'To give to Santa Claus,' said Daddy. 'You have to pay to go and see him. I'll wait for you here.'

Daddy stood rocking the twins in the pram, while Jeremy James joined the end of a long queue of children (Mummy was busy wasting time in the food department). Jeremy James thought it rather odd that you had to pay for Santa Claus. It was as if Santa Claus was a bar of chocolate or a packet of liquorice all-sorts.

'Do we really have to pay 50p to see him?' he asked a tall boy in front of him.

'Yeah,' said the tall boy. 'An' he'll prob'ly give you a plastic car worth 5p.'

Jeremy James stood on tiptoe to try and catch a glimpse of Father Christmas. He could just see him,

all wrapped up in his red cloak and hood, talking to a little girl with pigtails. It certainly was him – there was no mistaking the long white beard and the rosy cheeks. It was really quite an honour that Santa Claus should have come to this particular shop out of all the shops in the world, and perhaps he needed the 50p to help pay for his long journey. Jeremy James looked across towards his Daddy, and they gave each other a cheery wave.

As Jeremy James drew closer to Santa Claus, he felt more and more excited. Santa Claus seemed such a nice man. He was talking to each of the children before he gave them their present, and he would pat them on the head and sometimes let out a jolly laugh, and only once did he seem at all un-Father-Christmas-like; that was when a little ginger-haired boy with freckles stepped up before him and said he hadn't got 50p but he wanted a present all the same. Then Father Christmas pulled a very serious face and Jeremy James distinctly heard him ask the boy if he would like a thick ear, which seemed a strange sort of present to offer. The boy wandered off grumbling, and when he was some distance away stuck his tongue out at Santa Claus, but by then the next child was on the platform and the jolly smile had returned as the hand reached out for the 50p piece.

Jeremy James noticed, with a slight twinge of disappointment, that the presents really were rather small, but as Santa Claus had had to bring so many, perhaps he simply hadn't had room for bigger ones. It was still quite exciting to look at the different shapes and the different wrappings and try to guess what was inside them, and by the time Jeremy James came face to face with the great man, his eyes were shining and his heart was thumping with anticipation.

'What's your name?' asked Santa Claus in a surprisingly young voice.

'Jeremy James,' said Jeremy James.

'And have you got 50p for Santa Claus?'

'Yes,' said Jeremy James, handing it over.

Then Santa Claus gave a big smile, and his blue eyes twinkled out from below his bushy white eyebrows, and Jeremy James could see his shining white teeth between the bushy white moustache and the bushy white beard. All the bushy whiteness looked remarkably like cotton wool, and the redness on the cheeks looked remarkably like red paint, which made Jeremy James feel that Santa Claus really was very different from everybody else he knew.

'Is it for your reindeer?' asked Jeremy James.

'What?' asked Santa Claus.

'The 50p,' said Jeremy James.

'Ah,' said Santa Claus, 'ah well . . . in a kind of a sort of a manner of speaking as you might say. Now then Jeremy James, what do you want for Christmas?'

'Oh, I'd like a tricycle, with a bell *and* a saddlebag. Gosh, is that what you're going to give me?'

'Ah no, not exactly,' said Santa Claus, 'not now anyway. Not for 50p, matey. But here's a little something to keep you going.' And Santa Claus handed him a little oblong packet wrapped in Father-Christmassy paper.

'Thank you,' said Jeremy James. 'And do you really live in the North Pole?'

'Feels like it sometimes,' said Santa Claus. 'My landlord never heats the bedrooms. Off you go. Next!'

Jeremy James carried his little packet across to where Mummy had joined Daddy to wait with the twins.

'Open it up then,' said Daddy.

Jeremy James opened it up. It was a little box. And inside the little box was a plastic car.

'Worth at least 2p,' said Daddy.

'Five,' said Jeremy James.

Jeremy James's second meeting with Santa Claus came a week and a day later. It was at a children's party in the church hall. The party began with the Reverend Cole hobbling on to the platform and saying several times in his creaky voice that he hoped everyone would enjoy himself, and the party was to end with Santa Claus coming and giving out the presents. In between, there were games, eating and drinking, and more games. As soon as the first lot of games got underway, the Reverend Cole hobbled out of the hall, and nobody even noticed that he'd gone. The games were very noisy and full of running around, and as Jeremy James was extremely good at making a noise and running around, he enjoyed himself.

The eating and drinking bit came next, and Jeremy James showed that he was just as good at eating and drinking as he was at making a noise and running around. In fact Mummy, who was one of the helpers (having left Daddy at home to mind the twins and the television set), actually stopped him when he was on the verge of breaking the world record for the number of mince pies eaten at a single go. When at last there was not a crumb left on any of the tables, the helpers cleared the empty paper plates and the empty paper cups and the not so empty wooden floor. After a few more games full of shrieks and squeaks and bumps and thumps, all the children had completely forgotten about Santa Claus, but Santa Claus had not forgotten them. At the stroke of six o'clock, one of the grown-ups called for everyone to keep quiet and stand still, and at ten past six, when everyone was quiet and standing still, the hall door opened, and in came Father Christmas.

The first thing Jeremy James noticed about Father Christmas was how slowly he walked – as if his body was very heavy and his legs very weak. He was wearing the same red coat and hood as before, and he had a white beard and moustache, but ... somehow they were not nearly as bushy. His cheeks were nice and red, but . . . he was wearing a pair of spectacles. And when he called out to the children: 'Merry Christmas, everyone, and I hope you're enjoying yourselves!' his voice was surprisingly creaky and hollow-sounding.

Jeremy James frowned as Santa Claus heaved himself and his sack up on to the platform. There was definitely something strange about him. The other children didn't seem to notice, and they were all excited as the helpers made them line up, but perhaps the others had never met Santa Claus before, so how could they know?

Jeremy James patiently waited for his turn, and when it came, he stepped confidently up on to the platform.

'Now . . . er . . . what's your name?' said Santa Claus, peering down at Jeremy James.

'You should remember,' said Jeremy James. 'It was only a week ago that I told you.'

'Oh dear,' said Santa Claus. 'I do have a terrible memory.'

'And a week ago,' said Jeremy James, 'you weren't wearing glasses, and your voice wasn't all creaky like it is now.'

'Oh,' said Santa Claus, 'wasn't I . . . er . . . was it?'

Jeremy James looked very carefully at Santa Claus's face, and Santa Claus looked back at Jeremy James with a rather puzzled expression in his . . . brown eyes.

'Santa Claus has blue eyes!' said Jeremy James.

'Oh!' said Santa Claus, his mouth dropping open in surprise.

'And he's got white teeth, too!' said Jeremy James.

'Hm!' said Santa Claus, closing his mouth in dismay.

'You're not Santa Claus at all,' said Jeremy James. 'You're not!'

And so saying, Jeremy James turned to the whole crowd of children and grown-ups, and announced at the top of his voice:

'He's a cheat! He's not Father Christmas!'

Father Christmas rose unsteadily to his feet, and as he did so, his hood fell off, revealing a shining bald head. Father Christmas hastily raised a hand to pull the hood back on, but his hand brushed against his beard and knocked it sideways, and as he tried to save his beard, he brushed against his moustache, and that fell off altogether, revealing beneath it the face of . . . the Reverend Cole.

'There!' said Jeremy James. 'That proves it!'

One or two of the children started crying, but then the man who had been organising the games jumped up on to the platform and explained that the real Santa Claus was very busy preparing for Christmas, and that was why the Reverend Cole had had to take his place. They hadn't wanted to disappoint the children. And it was just bad luck that there'd been such a clever little boy at the party, but the clever little boy should be congratulated all the same on being so clever, and if they could just go on pretending that the Reverend Cole was the real Santa Claus, the clever little boy should have two presents as a special reward for being so clever.

Then the Reverend Cole put on his beard and moustache and hood again, and everybody clapped very loudly as Jeremy James collected his two

presents. And they were big presents, too – a book of bible stories, and a set of paints and brushes. As Jeremy James said to Mummy on the way home:

'It's funny that the real Santa Claus only gave me a rotten old car for 50p, but Mr Cole gave me these big presents for nothing.'

But as Father Christmas was a grown-up, and the Reverend Cole was also a grown-up, Jeremy James knew there was no point in trying to understand it all. Grown-ups never behave in the way you'd expect them to.

Waiting for Christmas

'The trouble with Christmas,' said Jeremy James, 'is the time in between.'

'In between what?' said Mummy, tinselling the Christmas tree.

'Well, in between whenever it is and Christmas,' said Jeremy James. 'Like in between today and Christmas. If there wasn't time in between, it would be Christmas now, and I wouldn't have to wait for my presents.'

'Ouch!' said Daddy, sticking a pin into a paper chain and a thumb. 'Blooming pins . . . never go where you want them to go.'

It was ever such a long time before Christmas – in fact a whole week. The world outside was like a giant birthday cake, covered with icing-snow, candle-trees, and houses made of candy. People walking down the street were all muffled up, showing nothing but their red cheeks and their shining eyes and their steam-engine puffs of breath. Inside, it was cosy and warm, and Mummy had been busy bathing and feeding the twins, cleaning the house, cooking the lunch and decorating the Christmas tree, while Daddy had been putting up a paper chain. Paper chains were difficult things to put up. Especially when Daddy was putting them up. They seemed to have minds of their own when Daddy put them up: while he stuck one end to the wall, the other end would curl round his arm and

his neck, so that he could only straighten it out by
unsticking the end he had stuck, but then when he'd
unstuck that end, it would also twine round his other
arm, and he would finish up by having to break the
paper chain in the middle in order to find his arms
again. Daddy didn't like paper chains, and paper
chains didn't seem too fond of Daddy.

'Mummy,' said Jeremy James. 'Daddy's sucking his
thumb again.'

'I can see we shall have to put another plaster on
it,' said Mummy.

'Pin went practically right through it,' said Daddy.
'Another millimetre and you could have put me in
somebody's butterfly collection.'

'Well,' said Mummy, 'let's hope you'll recover in
time to get that paper chain up before Christmas.'

'How far away *is* Christmas?' asked Jeremy James.

'Just ten minutes less than when you last asked,' said Mummy. 'A week, dear. Seven days and seven nights.'

'Well I don't think I can wait that long,' said Jeremy James. 'They should make it come earlier.'

'You can have your presents tomorrow if you like,' said Daddy. 'Only won't you be disappointed next week, when everybody else is getting presents and you're getting nothing!'

'You could have yours, too!' said Jeremy James.

'No thank you,' said Daddy. 'Otherwise we'll finish up celebrating the New Year with Easter eggs.'

Jeremy James was bursting to give Mummy and Daddy their presents. He wanted to give them their presents almost as much as he wanted them to give him his. He had saved up for ages and ages, and had given a great deal of thought to these presents, and he had bought them today all by himself at the sweet shop round the corner. Now they were nestling in a very secret place where no one would ever dream of looking: under his bed. There were two presents – one, a bright box of liquorice all-sorts with a robin on it, and the other, a thick bar of chocolate with Santa Claus on it. And the only problem Jeremy James had with these two perfect presents was to decide which one he should give to whom. He could easily imagine Mummy opening the bright box and saying, 'Here, Jeremy James, have a liquorice all-sort.' But he could just as easily imagine her breaking the thick bar of chocolate and saying, 'Here, Jeremy James, have a piece of chocolate.' On the other hand, he could hear Daddy saying, 'Here, Jeremy James, have some liquorice all-sorts,' But Daddy would also say, 'Here,

Jeremy James, have some chocolate.' It was a very difficult decision indeed.

Mummy's Christmas tree was looking more and more like an enchanted forest, and Daddy's paper chain was looking more and more like confetti. It might be best to concentrate on Mummy. There were two things Jeremy James wanted to know: would Mummy prefer chocolate or liquorice all-sorts, and what was Jeremy James getting for Christmas? They were very easy questions for Mummy to answer, but Jeremy James knew from experience that grown-ups didn't like answering questions. For instance, he'd asked Mummy how the twins had got into her stomach, but she hadn't told him, though she must have known because, after all, it was *her* stomach. And he'd asked Daddy how much money he'd got, but Daddy hadn't told him, though he must have known because, after all, it was *his* money. Grown-ups are very quick at asking you and ordering you and stopping you and starting you, but when it comes to answering you, they can be very slow indeed.

'Mummy,' said Jeremy James, casually poking a holly berry with his toe, 'which do you think is nicer, chocolate or liquorice all-sorts?'

'They're both nice,' said Mummy.

'Yes, but which is *nicer*?' said Jeremy James.

'Well, sometimes chocolate, and sometimes liquorice all-sorts,' said Mummy. 'It depends what you feel like.'

'Which do *you* usually feel like?' said Jeremy James.

Mummy thought long and hard. 'Well,' she said, 'in the afternoons, liquorice all-sorts, and in the evenings chocolate.'

Grown-ups can be quite exasperating at times. Jeremy James made one more effort: 'What about the mornings?'

'In the mornings,' said Mummy, 'I don't really feel like sweets at all.'

Jeremy James wandered over to Daddy.

'Daddy,' he said, 'which do you prefer – chocolate or liquorice all-sorts?'

Daddy seemed quite pleased to see Jeremy James, and he stopped work at his paper chain in order to consider the question.

'Well,' he said, 'I prefer chocolate to those pink liquorice all-sorts with black in the middle, but I prefer those black liquorice all-sorts with white in the middle to chocolate. But by and large, all in all, and as a whole, I think I'd say it's fifty-fifty.'

Jeremy James's face became as long as Santa Claus's beard.

'Which do *you* prefer?' asked Daddy.

Jeremy James's face shortened again. 'That's easy,' he said. 'Both.'

Mummy had finished the Christmas tree, and it sparkled like diamonds and emeralds.

'I'll give you a hand with those paper chains now,' she said to Daddy.

'Thanks,' said Daddy. 'Blooming awkward things. You can't really do them on your own.'

'No, you can't,' said Mummy, with rather more emphasis on 'you' than on 'can't'.

Jeremy James put his hands in his pockets and wandered over to the living-room door. His first question had been well and truly non-answered, and there seemed little point in asking the second. 'Wait and see,' they'd say, or 'You'll know on Christmas Day.' But at the last moment, he decided to ask it all the same.

'What *am* I going to have for Christmas?' he said.

'Wait and see,' said Daddy.

'You'll know on Christmas Day,' said Mummy.

Grown-ups are very predictable.

And Daddy went on showing Mummy how paper chains *should* be put up, and then Mummy started showing Daddy how paper chains *could* be put up. Jeremy James wandered out of the room and up the stairs. He peeped into the twins' room, but Christopher and Jennifer were both fast asleep, and even if they hadn't been fast asleep, they wouldn't have been able to help him. Babies weren't much help to anybody. All they could do was eat, sleep, cry and bring up wind. And make their nappies dirty. Babies, as far as Jeremy James was concerned, were a dead loss, and he couldn't see why grown-ups made such a fuss of them.

Jeremy James went into his own room, knelt down, and pulled two packets out from under the bed. There was no doubt about it, they were very attractive packets, and it made your mouth water just to look at them. It would make your mouth water even more to look at what was inside the packets. Mummy and Daddy were in for a real treat at Christmas. You couldn't have a nicer treat than chocolate and liquorice all-sorts. Unless, of course, there was something *wrong* with the chocolate and the liquorice all-sorts. For instance, the chocolate people might have accidentally wrapped up a block of wood by mistake, and the liquorice all-sorts people might have filled the

box with pebbles or marbles by mistake. These things do happen sometimes. Mummy had once found a piece of string in her soup, and Daddy was always finding little insects in his Brussels sprouts, and if the soup people and the Brussels sprout people can make mistakes like that, who knows what the chocolate people and the liquorice all-sort people might get up to? It was definitely safer for Jeremy James to have a quick look at what was *inside* the packets.

Inside the chocolate wrapper there was chocolate. Thick, dark, smooth-looking chocolate, with ridges in between the squares where you could break bits off. Jeremy James wondered if the chocolate would taste as nice as it looked. You could never tell by the way things looked. After all, when he'd had a cough a few weeks ago, Mummy had brought out a bottle with a lovely-looking red liquid in it, but the lovely-looking red liquid had tasted all ug-yuk-yurky, and he'd have spat it out if Mummy hadn't made him swallow it. No, you could never be sure that nice-looking things tasted nice. The only way to be sure was to try them for yourself. And you could always fold the silver paper over afterwards, to hide the bit that was missing . . . And no one would notice if there were two or three liquorice all-sorts missing from the box, because all the other liquorice all-sorts would roll together and fill the gap . . . The chocolate and the liquorice all-sorts did taste nice – in fact, they tasted delicious. All of them.

That night, which was just a week before Christmas, Jeremy James had a very bad tummy ache. Nobody else in the family had a tummy ache but, as Daddy said, it could just have been the excitement. Fortunately he was quite all right again after a couple of days, but every so often Mummy and Daddy noticed a slightly worried look on Jeremy James's face – especially when the talk came round to the subject of Christmas presents. But by Christmas Eve the worried frown had completely disappeared, and Jeremy James simply could not stop talking about Christmas presents. He couldn't wait to get his presents, and he couldn't wait to give his presents, and he wished time wouldn't pass so slowly, and he wouldn't sleep tonight, but he'd wait up for Santa Claus, and he wished he knew what Santa Claus was going to bring him, and would Mummy and Daddy like to know what Jeremy James had got them? He could tell them now if they liked. And he wouldn't mind if they told him what they were going to give him. He wouldn't mind giving *and* getting his presents straight away. No? Tomorrow? Oooooh, all right, then. But supposing tomorrow didn't come?

Tomorrow came, and it was the best Christmas there had ever been. Santa Claus had left a whole lot of apples and oranges and picture-books and toys and sweets in Jeremy James's empty pillow-case, and he'd left more toys and nice clothes for the twins, and when Jeremy James went down to the living-room – which was like fairyland with that sparkling tree and all those firmly fastened paper chains – he found an enormous parcel at the foot of the tree. Inside, there was the shiniest new tricycle with a bell *and* a saddlebag. But the most unusual presents were the presents Jeremy James gave his Mummy and Daddy. For Mummy there was a beautiful box with a pretty little robin on its lid. And inside the box were lots of pebbles, which Jeremy James had very carefully picked up at the bottom of the garden. And for Daddy there was a beautiful packet with a smiling Santa Claus on top and silver paper underneath, and inside the packet was a lovely block of wood (found in Daddy's tool-shed) with a picture of Daddy on it, drawn by Jeremy James himself. And although Mummy did make a little sound rather like 'Hmmph' when she first saw the box and Daddy's packet, she and Daddy smiled at each other, gave Jeremy James a big thank-you kiss, and agreed that, without a doubt, their presents had been well worth waiting for.

The Christmas Spirit

'The trouble with Christmas,' said Jeremy James, 'is the time after.'

'The time after what?' said Mummy, undressing the Christmas tree.

'After Christmas,' said Jeremy James.

'I though it was the time in between,' said Daddy, struggling to unravel himself from a paper chain which seemed reluctant to be taken down.

'No, the time in between's all right really,' said Jeremy James, 'because you can look forward to getting your presents then. Only with the time after, you can't look forward any more.'

'That's true,' said Daddy, 'unless you look forward to *next* Christmas.'

'That's too long,' said Jeremy James.

'Like this blooming paper chain,' said Daddy. 'More like a boa-constrictor than a paper chain.'

'I think we should have Christmas every day,' said Jeremy James, 'so that we can enjoy ourselves all the time.'

'If it was Christmas every day,' said Mummy, 'there'd never be any work done.'

It was a typical grown-up remark. They seemed to think work was all that mattered, and playing and enjoying yourself were not important. Life was all meat, potatoes and cabbage to them, with a tiny dollop of ice cream if there was time. They didn't seem to realise that they were much *happier* playing games and giving one another presents, and Jeremy James was much happier too, and all they had to do was pretend every day was Christmas and they could live happily ever after. What was the point of working if it stopped you from enjoying yourself?

'Why do you have to do work?' said Jeremy James.

'Good question,' said Daddy. 'I sometimes ask myself the same thing.'

'Because if Daddy didn't work,' said Mummy, 'there'd be no money to pay for our house and our food and our clothes and everything else. And if I didn't work, you'd have nothing to eat and nothing to wear. You didn't like it when we went on strike, did you? And that's how it would be all the time.'

'Well, maybe you should just work every one day, and then have Christmas every next day,' said Jeremy James. 'That would be fair.'

Daddy agreed, and Mummy said perhaps they'd do that when their ship came home, and Jeremy James said he didn't know they had a ship, and Mummy said that was just another way of saying when they were very rich, and Daddy said it was another way of saying pigs would fly.

'Anyway,' said Daddy, 'I agree with Jeremy James. If we celebrated Christmas all the year round, people would be happier, the world would be brighter, and I wouldn't have to keep fighting these blooming paper chains.'

There was no doubt that Christmas was well and truly over. The turkey, Christmas pudding and mince pies were all finished, the decorations were coming down, the cards and parcels had stopped arriving, and even the crisp white snow had given way to dirty grey slush. It was as if the whole world had decided to be miserable. It made Jeremy James feel quite depressed, until he was suddenly struck by an interesting idea:

'Will the shops be open again now?' he asked.

'Yes,' said Mummy.

'Aha!' said Jeremy James. The interesting idea looked even more interesting. 'I've got some money upstairs,' said Jeremy James. 'Left over from Christmas.'

'Have you?' said Mummy.

'Yes,' said Jeremy James.

There was a moment's silence. Mummy didn't seem to have realised that Jeremy James had had an interesting idea.

'If the shops are open,' said Jeremy James, 'I could go and spend some of my money, couldn't I?'

'I haven't got time to go shopping now, dear,' said Mummy, who had finished taking decorations off the Christmas tree and was now taking decorations off Daddy.

'Well, can I just go to the sweetshop round the corner, then?' asked Jeremy James.

'Yes, I suppose so,' said Mummy. 'Only you'd better not spend more than 25p.'

That made the interesting idea a little less interesting than it had been, but still, you could buy a lot of nice sweets with 25p – 25p worth, in fact.

'Can I go on my new tricycle?' asked Jeremy James.

'As long as you don't go in the road,' said Mummy.

'It's pavement all the way,' said Daddy. 'But don't

go knocking down old ladies or garden walls, and don't break the speed limit.'

The interesting idea became an interesting reality. Jeremy James, muffled up in scarf and overcoat, slipped a few shining coins into his shining leather saddlebag, tinkled loudly on his shining silver bell, and set out through the splashy, squelchy, slithery slush to break the world tricycle record between home and the sweetshop. There was nobody on the pavement at all, and with a loud brrm brrm Jeremy James gathered speed, his legs whirling round like pink catherine wheels. As he neared the corner, he slowed down a little, swung the handlebars round, let out a loud 'errgh' worthy of any world champion driver, and raced headlong into a great mass of brown stuff that was all soft and crumply and made a noise very similar to Jeremy James's 'Errgh' only louder and deeper. When the soft crumply mass of brown stuff had picked itself up off the pavement, it turned out to be a man in a brown overcoat. The man in the brown overcoat wasn't too pleased at his first meeting with Jeremy James, and as he brushed the wet slush off himself, he looked rather fiercely at the tricycle and its rider, and said:

'You wanner look where you're goin' with that thing. I could 'ave bin killed. Dead.'

'I'm ever so sorry,' said Jeremy James. 'I didn't see you.'

'Not many people *can* see round corners,' said the man in the brown overcoat. 'That's why you should go slow round corners. So you don't bump into people an' kill 'em dead.'

The man in the brown overcoat was fairly old, and his coat was very old, because it was all torn and thready. When he'd stopped looking fiercely at Jeremy James, his face became kinder, though it was covered in spiky bristles and didn't seem very clean.

'Got that for Christmas, did you?' he said, nodding towards the tricycle.

'Yes,' said Jeremy James. 'And it's got a bell *and* a saddlebag.'

'So I see,' said the man. 'An' it's a nice solid job an' all, 'cause I felt 'ow solid it is. When a solid job like that bumps into somebody, the somebody can feel 'ow solid it is.'

The man in the brown overcoat sat down on a garden wall, and pulled a half-smoked cigarette out of his pocket. Jeremy James noticed that the man was wearing grey gloves which his fingers poked out of, and on the man's feet were some black shoes that his toes poked out of.

'Aren't your fingers and toes cold?' he asked the man.

'Don't know,' said the man. 'Can't feel 'em.'

'Well you should have asked Santa Claus to give you shoes and gloves for Christmas,' said Jeremy James. 'Only you're too late now.'

'Santa Claus never brings me nothin' anyway,' said the man. ''E don't 'ave time for people like me.'

'Do you mean you didn't get *any* Christmas presents?' said Jeremy James. 'Not even from your Mummy and Daddy?'

'That would 'ave bin a surprise,' said the man. 'They've bin dead twenty years. No, sonny, nobody gives presents to ole blokes like me. People either walk straight past you, or they knock you down.'

108

'I didn't *mean* to knock you down,' said Jeremy James. 'And I did say sorry.'

'I know that, son,' said the man. 'An' *you* stopped to talk to me, didn't you?'

The man puffed at his cigarette, and blew a little cloud of smoke into the air. He really was a very dirty man – his hair, his face, his clothes and even his fingernails were dirty.

'Why are you so dirty?' asked Jeremy James.

'Protection,' said the man. 'Dirt protects you against the cold, you see. Now if Santa Claus was to give me a nice warm house an' nice clean clothes, an' a nice warm Christmas dinner, I wouldn't need all this dirt.'

'I don't think Santa Claus gives that sort of present,' said Jeremy James. 'I think you have to do work to get that.'

'I expect you're right,' said the man. 'And that's why I'm so dirty.'

All the same, Jeremy James thought it a bit unfair that the man in the brown overcoat should have had no Christmas present at all, and a plan began to form in his mind. It was a plan that needed to be thought about a little, because after all 25p was 25p, but the thinking didn't last very long.

'Can you wait here for a minute?' asked Jeremy James.

'Well, I expect so,' said the man. 'I don't 'ave any urgent appointments for today.'

'Brrm brrm!' said Jeremy James, and pedalled at world record speed away from the man in the brown overcoat. 'I'll be back in a minute!' he called as he pedalled.

And back in a minute he was. With a loud 'Errgh!' he screeched to a halt right beside the man in the brown overcoat. Then Jeremy James got off his tricycle, and went to his saddlebag.

'Now close your eyes and hold out your hand,' he said to the man in the brown overcoat.

The man did as he was told, and when he opened his eyes again, he found that his hand was holding a completely full packet of liquorice all-sorts.

'It's a Christmas present,' said Jeremy James.

The man in the brown overcoat looked at the packet of liquorice all-sorts, then he looked at Jeremy James. Then he looked at the packet again, and then again at Jeremy James.

'What's your name, son?' he said at last.

'Jeremy James,' said Jeremy James.

'Well, Jeremy James,' said the man, 'it's the best Christmas present I've ever 'ad. An' if Jesus 'isself was to give me a present, it couldn't be better'n this one. I'll remember you, Jeremy James.'

Then the man in the brown overcoat stood up, and he patted Jeremy James gently on the head with a half-gloved hand.

'I must be on me way now. But I'll always remember you, Jeremy James.'

'Merry Christmas, then,' said Jeremy James.

'Merry Christmas to you, too,' said the man.

And the man walked slowly away in one direction, while Jeremy James brrm-brrmed at top speed in the other. There was, thought Jeremy James to himself, a great deal to be said for having Christmas every day.